MORPHED

ARTIS L. NELSON

Trilogy Christian Publishers
A Wholly Owned Subsidiary of Trinity Broadcasting Network
2442 Michelle Drive
Tustin, CA 92780

For information, address Trilogy Christian Publishing
Rights Department, 2442 Michelle Drive, Tustin, Ca 92780.
Trilogy Christian Publishing/ TBN and colophon are trademarks of Trinity Broadcasting Network.

For information about special discounts for bulk purchases, please contact Trilogy Christian Publishing.

Manufactured in the United States of America

10 9 8 7 6 5 4 3 2 1

Library of Congress Cataloging-in-Publication Data is available.

ISBN 978-1-64088-591-2 (Print Book)
ISBN 978-1-64088-592-9 (ebook)

DEDICATION

I dedicate this book to Henry Nelson, my grandpapa, whose earthly life profoundly influenced mine. He and my big mama, Willie-Mae Nelson, planted the spiritual seeds in our family, which opened the doors for further pursuit of God's purpose in our lives.

This book is also dedicated to my wife of twenty-one years, our children, and the many people who were instrumental in my complete freedom. People like Kenneth Copeland, who sent me a free book every month of my incarceration from his ministry. Thanks for doing it in a dignified way, allowing me to pick a book from a catalog after prayerfully considering what I needed next in my journey. You were definitely present in what God did in my life. Special thanks to Sam and Sally Severn, who sacrificed their time to help birth a lot of projects, including this book, which they labored for as if it came from their own experience. Every life that is impacted by this book will be added to the eternal inheritance of these people as well. Thanks for being a part of my story.

CONTENTS

INTRODUCTION

• • • • • •

Morph[1] |*môrf*|verb

> To change *"from one image to another by small gradual steps…to undergo or cause to undergo a gradual process of transformation"* ("Morph" 2019a). *"To change the form or character of: to transform"* ("Morph" 2019b).

How does a man morph?

How does he orchestrate transformation in his life?

How does he put aside his past, his crimes or failures, and discover his true purpose, his real identity?

Let's take the most extreme example we can think of. The most heinous, most repulsive human being our minds can conjure up. Let's say this human being, this man, is a convicted killer. Let's also make him a thief and a drug dealer—a violent, destructive man who has robbed, brutalized, and killed.

Can a bad man like that change? Can his evil past be transformed, turned around and saved by something bigger? Can his true purpose be revealed and restored? Can he be redeemed?

Most of us might say no.

But ask yourself: *What if?*

What if a man like that could change and find redemption? *What if* he could turn away from being destructive to himself and the world around him, and be transformed into a contributing member of society, a positive role model, a man committed to bettering his community—a healer, a helper, and a rescuer?

Still don't believe it's possible?

Then read on. I have a confession to make.

You see, I was that man.

But my story isn't one of crimes. My story is of transformation. It's a story of redemption, of hearing the wake-up call of God, of being morphed and changed by His loving hand.

My transformation story is unlike any other because it's real. It's raw. It's shocking.

And it's all true.

It's the story of two lives—my early thug life, stuck in a self-sabotaging cycle of sin, and my second morphed life.

In my first life, I was a young boy raised on the streets of Seattle. Like most children, I grew up with dreams. I dreamt of being an athlete, a rapper, someone who would be celebrated. At fourteen, I was stealing motorcycles and cars. I moved into a dope house at seventeen, and thus began the character traits of someone who would be considered, later in life, a seasoned criminal. At age twenty-seven, I was on trial for first-degree murder.

I wasn't convicted of those charges, but I did have to surrender to the ugly truth. Either I could continue down this evil path, and die like a caged animal behind bars, or I could surrender to God's call on my life, let Him drive out this dysfunction, and find a new life and my true identity in Christ.

In my second life—the brand-new life God's grace granted me—I became a pastor, a shepherd, a Christ-follower, a loving husband and father, and the man He created me to be. It was in my second life that I discovered my true identity.

Tears well up in my eyes, just writing those words. It's when I think back to my early childhood that the humbling grace of God and His ultimate plan for my life really clicks into clarity.

When I look back into childhood, superheroes dominated my young thoughts. I wanted to be a real hero, like Iron Man, Spider-Man, or Superman. Those made-up comic-book characters were real to me because they could transform from normal, everyday individuals into heroes, supernaturally gifted saviors. Superman would actually go to a secret place, a phone booth, and in that secret place morph from normal, weak Clark Kent into a man who could fly, whose paranormal powers could save the world.

Those superhero stories dominated my childhood. They whispered a secret truth to me that each of us has the potential to change, to be morphed from one thing to another. But that's Marvel and DC Comics—the truth is, it's not *real*.

How does a *real* flesh and blood man—a man or woman like you and I—morph?

Simply put: By God's grace. By shifting the lens of our perspective to focus on fulfilling God's great purpose for us. By letting Jesus make us new. There is no other way.

I see you nodding your head in agreement. I bet your story is a lot like mine—a constant battle with insecurities, self-doubts, and spiritual inconsistencies, wondering if you are living a life that is pleasing to God.

Like you, my story is one of forgiveness. And it's a daily battle, a fight, a spiritual rumble-in-the-jungle. It's the struggle to recognize that we all have the potential to become more than conquerors and overcomers, given spiritual power by the Blood of the Lamb, the same power that raised Jesus Christ from the dead. It's a story filled with broken pieces, terrible choices, and ugly facts. It's also filled with amazing comebacks and an enormous grace that saved my life when all was lost.

That's how I morphed. God granted me a miracle—the opportunity to walk away from a criminal life, to walk in the cleansing light of His love, to triumph over the evil locked inside me, and start over. He granted me the opportunity to surrender myself and to write this book with one purpose:

To morph *you.*

God's awesome love is big enough and mighty enough to do that. Through God's love, we can receive forgiveness for our sins. We can find hope in the dark.

God's love can transform you and change you. All you need to do is let Him free you from guilt and shame, and morph you into the marvelous, one-of-a-kind creation He constructed you to be.

How does a man morph?

Read on. And through my story, I'll show you.

CHAPTER ONE

• • • • • •

THE HURT AND THE DIRT

Boom! The cell door slammed shut, awakening me. Slowly I gazed around the dim room. I was on a bare mattress, tucked into the corner, surrounded by four concrete walls. Near my head sat a filthy, vomit-splattered toilet, made of indestructible stainless steel. Outside the room, angry men hooted and hollered, and a voice blasted over the PA, "Ten minutes until count time! Be on your bunks!"

Where am I? I dizzily thought to myself. *Is this a dream?* My heart pounded and hammered. Burrowing beneath my itchy wool blanket, I closed my eyes and curled up in a fetal position. The room was freezing. For some reason, they were piping in bitterly cold air through the vents, and the plexiglass slot on the cell window was stuck open so that icy wind came whistling and roaring in.

The freezing air chilled me. Unable to sleep, I climbed out of my bunk, stretched, and exercised to try and get the blood pumping through the rest of my body to stay warm. Finally, I gave up, and burrowed under my itchy blanket again, staring at my cell door, waiting for it to open.

I'm still here, I reminded myself.

I lay there, freezing cold, rubbing the goosebumps on my arms. Above and below me, I heard the enraged shouts of other inmates on my block. On both sides of the tier, men were screaming and yelling back and forth, fishing things across the tier and asking if they received it, making it impossible for my mind to find peace, solitude, or to delve into my inner thoughts.

The screaming was so loud, I couldn't think. I tried to center myself and block out all the noise, but the familiar howls and shrieks of the other convicts surrounded me. Hurling off my blanket, I leaped up and paced my 6' x 9' cell. The ugly voices were a recurring presence, impossible to ignore, and they filled me with an aggressive, violent feeling. Silently I debated whether to join in the screaming and cursing by chipping in a few choice words of my own.

Louder and louder, the screaming grew. Blood rushed to my skull. Anger washed over me so strong, I could hardly breathe. Mentally exhausted, I choked down my anger and crawled back into my bunk, waiting for the guards to arrive, waiting for the count time.

Lying alone in my icy room, I clamped my eyes closed, trying to shut out the clanging cell doors and the howling voices, forced to turn inward. As I turned inward, I began to question myself. *How did I get here? Who am I? What am I doing here?*

Jarred by another steel cell door slamming shut, the sound deafening, I suddenly remembered: *I'm here because I'm like the rest of these guys. Violent. With no respect for my own life or the lives around me. Numb to pain and ready to inflict pain on the world.*

I'm burnt out.

A gangbanger, the first chief of the biggest, deadliest street gang in the area.

I'm a man who stole, brutalized, and butchered.
And I'm a convict.

My head was crawling with questions. My prison shirt was a sweaty mass of wrinkles. In that moment, surrounded by the cries of Class-A felons, robbers, serial killers, and rapists, I felt like the trash that I was, a piece of human garbage, lower than the lowliest creature on the face of the earth.

I felt like dirt.

Locked in my prison cell, shivering under the icy breeze blasting in through the window, it was as if I was wearing that same shame. Caged in here, like a ferocious, bloodthirsty beast, I was that dangerous dealer people ran from on the streets. Still, something inside of me was crying out. It was almost as if the innocent little boy I'd been was there, seated beside me in my cell, the child I'd been before my behavior transformed me into a callous and cold-hearted criminal.

My life was supposed to turn out different. *You're not supposed to be here,* I repeated over and over to myself. Once upon a time, I was an innocent child, who could have been anybody, who could have done anything. Instead, I was here—a prisoner.

I lay down on my dingy bed, wishing I was invisible. On the outside, I was a brutal, six foot three inches tall, two-hundred-fifty-pound, aggressive young man who had disgraced himself and his family. On the inside was a little boy who'd been held captive inside this violent individual, a boy who once pursued dreams and goals, a boy screaming and crying to be set free.

Fell on Black Days

As I lay there in that cold place, where sunlight couldn't be seen, I noticed there was a little paperback book on the side of the cell that a past resident had been reading. I picked it up. It was a book by Kenneth E. Hagin, called *The Triumphant Church.*

What kind of stuff are these guys looking at? I thought to myself.

Out of boredom, I cracked the little book open and started flipping pages. I wanted to escape into the pages of a book, or escape inside of an imagination that was different from the environment I'd been penned in.

I kept flipping pages. And I began to read.

I read only a little bit before my eyes widened. I stopped and set the book down. Suddenly, I noticed I was sweating bullets. In a flash, my mind went deeper inward. I began to look at who I really was as a youngster. I looked back at my childhood, and the trajectory my life had been forced into. Looking back into childhood, I let my memory fill in the blanks. I remembered what that young boy was going through, dealing with overwhelmingly destructive family issues.

I grew up experiencing physical and verbal abuse starting at a young age. By the time I was fifteen, I had grown numb to the pain. What saved me from being devoured by my situation was the two superheroes I loved as a child.

I loved The Incredible Hulk and Superman. Both characters were inspiring to me because they changed from normal, everyday men into supernatural beings, blessed with incredible power. What inspired me about The Hulk was the way he *transformed.* The Hulk would experience anger and unleash that anger, morphing from a meek scientist Bruce Banner into a powerful, raging monster. He'd morph from a weak little man into a green beast who could destroy and crush anything in his path. He had controlled anger. Super endowed with unbelievable strength by his rage; there was no power on earth that could stop The Hulk.

Seeing how a man could morph gave me hope. The Hulk's story seemed like a personal message, just to me. It fueled my dreams that I could conquer my struggles and that a transformation was possible.

Holding that Kenneth Hagin book in my hand, and thinking back on those old times, I felt alone and vulnerable. I stared the little book down as if it was interrogating me, cross-examining me, accusing me. Then I lay my head down on the mattress and climbed inside the thoughts of my childhood.

I started to feel sick, very sick. Desperately I wanted to spill my guts to somebody. Once, I could be anything I wanted. I had dreams. I had hoped. But now those old dreams seemed planted in my past.

Part of me always embraced the darkness in my soul. It baffled me that I'd allowed myself to sabotage those dreams, that my life had fallen on black days, and reached a dead end. Why? Because I had an appetite for destruction. An appetite for the hurt and the dirt.

I felt this aching sensation in my belly, as I imagined my life eating itself.

From the day I was put out on the streets at seventeen, I operated on one power source—*fear.* The Lord knows I didn't desire to be evil. But I gained everything I had through violence. When I first became homeless, I learned that to be feared was the equivalent of being valued. Where I was from, fear was a weapon we wielded. Fear had power. Fear manipulated. Fear terrorized. Fear paralyzed people into action and crashed open doors.

Back in my cell, my stomach turned. I knew I was a bad man. More violent. More aggressive. More ruthless. More brutal.

It was all too much for me to bear. I felt trapped in some horrible dream, one I couldn't wake from. For minutes I lay shaking on my bunk, clutching that little book, flinching at every door slam I heard.

I was at the lowest point of my life—rock bottom. I had become an animal, a threat to the community, a danger to my friends and family, to everybody and everything I came into contact with.

I'm not human, I said to myself, my heart racing. Tormented by shame, my gaze fixated on those four concrete walls, my thoughts bleeding one into the next, fear running wild in my brain.

What did I do?

I sat up, putting my head between my knees. Desperately seeking answers, with every new thought, my hope continued to fade. Even thoughts of escaping prison left my mind. And yet if I stayed here, I was going to die like a beast in a cage. I was forced to make a genuine decision as to who I would be in the minutes to follow.

Erasing My Warped Ways

At that moment, the announcement of "count time!" jarred me. I leaped up and paced my cell, my brain pounding, my mind spinning. Disappointment and depression hit me, like a freight train.

I kept going back to my childhood, trying to find my true identity. I thought about winning spelling bees as a kid and being the smart kid in my classroom. I thought about writing stories and drawing superheroes and all the happy things I did as a youngster.

I tried to pinpoint the moment I changed from a boy who could be anything to a thug who grabbed and destroyed everything in his path, who would end up locked in a prison cell. I felt unworthy. Undeserving of redemption. Fearful that it was too late to be saved.

As worry
Kenneth Hag
starting-over
ways that k
    Cor
    C
    (

ke'
in
dark
wanted—a

I knew I co
same violent man, to be
I could surrender myself to ne.
myself, of doing things, and endure u.
could experience the pain and suffering of s.

I could choose either of these paths. This was
to choose a new direction. To change, to be transformed
morph, like the superheroes I so revered.

And yet, I hesitated. I didn't know how to get there. I
didn't know if I'd *ever* get there, or if the change I craved was
worth fighting for.

Suddenly, the cold air whistling through the cell window bit into my bones. I was hit by another wave of hope-
lessness. I wrestled with the fear, surprised by my renewed
mental strength, holding onto a hope that seemed to come
out of nowhere, a hope that was miraculously real, a hope
whose voice grew louder and louder in my ears.

"*Don't worry,*" the voice inside me seemed to whisper.
"*Let go. And trust me.*"

I dropped my head.

I clutched the book to my chest.

ARTIS L. N

I closed my eyes, took
and said a silent prayer.
I prayed for mercy.
forgive me, for all the
Then I paused
my heart, I made
to change, to pu
ever lay on the
was necessar
I open
within
Su
I k

a deep breath, let it slowly out,

I prayed for real change, for God to hurt I'd caused.

and took one more deep breath. And in a commitment. A vow to be transformed, sh through, and seek out and accept what-other side of change, to endure whatever pain y for my complete redemption.

ed the door to God, to Jesus, my Savior.

denly, I felt tidal waves of confidence swelling me.

I thought about my future. I thought about my family. ew if I made the decision to commit wholeheartedly, no atter how bad it hurt, no matter how the outside world beat against me, I would do all that was required for change, and I would stay to the end.

Whatever old excuses I'd offered were insufficient, whatever made-up reasons I'd told myself were suddenly exposed as lies.

I was ready for change.

In cell number nine that day, in the bowels of a prison, I made a tearful vow to myself. Not just to turn away from toxic influences. Not just to stop the pollution of my soul. Not just to stop poisoning my relationships. Not just to pursue God. Not just to pursue change. But to commit to a penetrating *change* that could come only from God. A *change* that not only would allow Godly character to be formed in me but through me for Him to affect the world around me.

I committed to giving Him the same intensity or more than I gave in my pursuits of evil. I turned myself over in complete surrender to wholeheartedly pursuing a relationship with God. And the work began...

CHAPTER TWO

· · ● · ·

HOW MY IDENTITY BROUGHT ON ADVERSITY

My battle to fight my old wicked ways, to wrestle with self-doubt, and surrender to God's change, began that day. Though my heart melted in fear of change, I knew it was time. Time to be honest with myself. Time to come clean and peel away my old reputation. Time to find the new identity given to me by God. The Lord, Himself, had placed me on a mission to prove that He will intervene even in the lives of the worst among us—even in the life of a former gangbanger, drug dealer, and convict like me—if we'll do one thing:

Listen.

On the Run From God

After an act of evil in my past, all I could see in every direction was doom surrounding me. I went on the run. Dodging the police, I caught a Greyhound bus heading to California. I'd been scheduled to attend the Billboard Awards in Los Angeles the following week, as I had been signed to a record company and was releasing my first rap single, *Blame it on the Drink.*

Because I ended up arriving early, I stayed at a hotel in Studio City rather than at my record company executive's house. I holed up there, alone, isolated, wracked by waves of foreboding thoughts. My future was a wide-open passage leading nowhere. I was exhausted, yet every cell in my body felt like it was on fire.

I collapsed on the hotel mattress and dissolved into what seemed like instant replays continuously looping in my head. I hadn't slept in four days. Furious with myself, I kept reliving the bad decisions, savoring the brutality of my actions. But my anger soon cooled, and I started plotting what I'd do next.

Straining my worn-out mind, I concluded there were seven people I needed to eliminate. I knew removing them was my best option to stop a war from escalating into endangering my family. Bubbling with adrenaline, I pictured myself holding my MAK-90 with the 75-round Tommy-gun clip in it, catching my adversaries off-guard and snatching their very souls.

I later learned what was happening back home. My mother and auntie had been praying over me for the past forty-eight hours, begging and pleading with God to intervene after the police had surrounded my mother's house on a manhunt for me. It was at this critical juncture then that I finally drifted into a deep sleep and was plunged into a dramatic dream.

It was a dream, unlike any I'd ever experienced. I saw myself outside of my own body, looking down at myself from the sky, watching events as they occurred. I watched my dream-self walk into a Greyhound bus station with a ticket heading back to Seattle. As I approached the line for the bus, I strolled up behind a guy in a leather biker jacket. In front of him stood a thin, cheap blue fabric suitcase, like the one my mother owned long ago. On the front of the suitcase was the stitched-in initial "N".

Suddenly the dream skipped—like a movie fast-forwarding—and I saw myself on the bus, asleep. Hovering in mid-air like an angel, I watched the Greyhound bus drive underneath. I peered down and saw my slumbering head leaned against the vehicle's window. I saw myself wake and yawn and look outside, my darkly ringed eyes landing upon a restaurant with neon lights glowing. I stared at the glimmering restaurant, then like a shot I awoke from the dream.

I roused, feeling strange, feeling puzzled. As the dream faded and I got myself together, a young woman from Vegas appeared to drive me to Baldwin Hills. Years before, this young lady worked for me when I was running escort services.

As I climbed into her car, my head was still buzzing from the strangeness of that dream. Weaving through traffic and the bustling city streets, we drove past strip malls, massage parlors, and pawn shops. After a slow glide around town, the car banked a corner, and sitting in front of us was the Greyhound bus station.

"Stop! Turn in here!" I suddenly blurted out. I sounded manic. Staring at me like I must be crazy, the woman hit the brakes and wheeled into the parking lot.

With big eyes, I gazed at the bus terminal, my mind whirling. Anxiety crept up my spine. I closed my eyes and breathed, once, twice. Opening my eyes, I barely registered the young woman regarding me. I lowered my voice, trying to understand what was happening. "Go inside the Greyhound station," I told her, "and buy me a ticket back to Seattle."

"What?" The woman looked jarred, befuddled. "Why are you getting a bus ticket back to Seattle? I thought you were here for the Billboard Awards."

"Go get me a ticket," I said again, nagging fear pounding in my chest and my heart beating like cardiac arrest was approaching if I rejected this choice.

The woman rolled her eyes, sighed. She had no idea what I had been through, nor that I was on the run—as far as she knew, I was preparing for an awards show. Dumbfounded, she trudged into the station. Minutes later, she came out holding my ticket.

I felt my heart quickening, my breathing fast and shallow. *What am I doing?* I thought. I suddenly felt an intense pressure on my heart—an internal force pushing me to go into the Greyhound station.

"Listen," I said, fighting off the sweats, "This is what I want you to do. You're going to call Demitri"—Demitri was the record company executive—"and you're going to tell him I'm not coming because I have to head back to Seattle, to take care of some business." Then I grabbed my bag and hurried off into the station.

My scalp tingling and itching, and my legs turned to lead; I approached the bus terminal. When I strolled into the Greyhound station, I climbed back into the dream. Almost detached, I watched myself. With my ticket in hand I walked up to the guy with the biker jacket on. In front of him stood the blue fabric suitcase with the initial "N". Shaken and scared by the sight of the bag, I stood in line to get on the bus. When I got on the bus, I dropped fast into a deep sleep.

During the bus ride north, my mind gave up control. I descended into the dream again. In the middle of the journey, my eyes at once snapped open, and I saw the glowing neon signs of a breakfast restaurant by the roadside. Certain I was losing my mind, my eyes searched the sky above the bus, looking for the angel-me from the dream. I saw nothing. Through a haze of shock and pain, I curled up in my seat, lost in a cloud of dream-soaked images infiltrating my brain. Checking off my mental list of what I intended to do next, and who I was going to do it too, I decided to get off the bus at Portland. I snatched up my bag and stuffed it under my arm and raced off to find the nearest liquor store and hotel.

By the time I reached the first hotel and was safely inside the door, I'd lost all sense of reality. I roamed down the corridors, which were completely empty. *I've got to get out of this hotel*, I thought, *and go to the Lloyd Center*—which is a mall there in Portland. *I've got to go watch a movie or something.*

I raced out the front door and caught a cab to Lloyd Center. Entering through the backside of the mall, my eyes adjusted to the bright lights, which seemed almost like a natural extension of the dream I was in. I coasted through the mall, rolling past this little Bible bookstore. When I looked in the bookstore, I thought to myself, *That's something my mom and my aunties and my grandma would like, all that little Bible stuff, trinkets, and things they could put on the refrigerator.* Continuing to wander the mall, I went into a magazine store across from the Bible bookstore, purchased a *Billboard* magazine, so I could check out the charts, then rode the escalator to get some food and see a movie.

At the mall courtyard, I scarfed down fistfuls of hot food. But for some reason, I couldn't taste it. My stomach muscles constricted and clenched into a fist. I was coming apart.

In a panic, I hurried to the movies. At that time, they had phone booths on the side of the theater. As I passed the phones, I experienced an echoing voice in my head, telling me, "Call your sister at work. Call your sister."

Sweat pearled on my scalp. I shook my head to rid it of the voice. *This is ridiculous!* I disregarded the words I'd heard, thinking, *I'm truly losing my mind.* I bought my ticket, picked out a seat and watched an entire movie, without seeing a single frame. The whole time, my mind was fixated on the evil I had done, and what I would do next. How I'd make sure all my enemies were erased. The longer I sat there, literally on the edge of my seat, my evil thoughts buzzed around each other.

Finally, the movie ended. I walked out, past the same phone booth again. Again I heard that invisible voice: "Call your sister at work." It sounded so real that I spoke out loud and replied, "I don't know her phone number!"

And then, as if out of earshot of everybody else, I heard it. I heard the phone number.

My sister Robin worked at the Port of Seattle Police. Robin was a security officer at the airport. Desperately, I put a quarter in the slot and dialed the number.

"Is Robin there?" I inquired, in a shaky voice. Seconds later, I heard my sister's voice over the phone. She was sobbing, ecstatic to hear from me. She told me the police had surrounded my mother's house and burst in brandishing guns, how the family was pursuing getting me an attorney, the best attorney in the state. She pleaded with me to call her in two days that she'd be able to tell me whatever was going on back home.

I hung up, overwhelmed. It all seemed like a joke. *This couldn't be happening, right?* Though I didn't know it at the time, the Spirit of God had been the motivating force behind the urge to call my sister, and God had given me her phone number.

For the moment, I felt profound relief. I believed I was going to make it out of this mess. Immediately I began to think there was a way of escape. *Maybe I don't have to do anything to the rest of those guys,* I reasoned. *Maybe they can live. Maybe I can live, too.*

When God Gets Involved

My thoughts unfolding in a blissful blur, I left the phone booth and rode back down the escalator, past the little Bible bookstore with my *Billboard* magazine in hand. Suddenly, I felt pressured to go into this store. *What for?* I wondered. I strode in, still thinking I had lost my mind. Rolling up to the clerk, and like I was still in the dream, I looked around and asked, "Hey, you got one of those books I can read?"

The words jarred me. I'd gone to church as a child. My grandfather was a deacon, a humble man who showed me what it was like to be a man of God. And my grandmother was partners with Oral Roberts Ministries. I remember her making me run back and forth to the mailbox out by the street to pick up her Oral Roberts Bible and her prayer request-response letters.

But that stuff wasn't real to me. It wasn't suited for me because I had gone off and acted a fool, and the folks I saw who were supposed to be Christians weren't really portraying what I thought Christianity was all about. So, as a teen, I chose to reject that.

Imagine my surprise when I walked into this bookstore and asked, "Do you have a Bible I can read?"

"Sure," the lady clerk said. She didn't gawk at me, just grabbed a NIV Bible off the shelf and handed it over. Dead with mental fatigue, I took the Bible and walked out.

Now, as I walked, thoughts popped up like mushrooms. I started analyzing everything. I analyzed the phone call to my sister. Analyzed my dream. I'd begun to think that maybe this was God who'd showed me to this bookstore, to the Greyhound station, and getting a ticket to Seattle. Maybe God had awakened me in the bus and showed me the neon restaurant signs. Maybe God told me my sister's phone number, so I could call her and she could tell me the family is about to get an attorney because they don't want to let the police shoot me down in the streets.

Perhaps—just perhaps—this isn't just crazy talk. *Perhaps, God is involved.*

Bombarded by this firestorm of thoughts, I returned to the hotel, ordered a pizza, drank some Very Superior Old Pale (VSOP) cognac I'd bought earlier, opened the *Billboard* magazine, and started looking at the charts. After a few minutes of reading, the magazine seemed to lose all sparkle. The sparkle returned as I thought about that Bible I'd purchased.

As I put down the magazine and brought the Bible up into my hands, the whole world seemed to light up. I felt a yearning, a rising in my spirit again, and the sudden need to take the plastic wrapper off the Bible. As if my fingers knew what they were doing, I ripped off the wrapper and opened the book to wherever it landed.

It happened to be Luke, chapter 15, the story of the *Prodigal Son.*

As I read, I felt like I was being identified as the *Prodigal Son.* I felt overwhelmed with a renewed vigor because God was looking for me, the lost son. I felt I was the lost coin in the story. Like I was the sheep, the coin, and the prodigal son who were all lost, but could find a way home.

All at once, a tremendous burst of peace and relief exploded in my brain. It was as if I broke on the inside. The words of Luke calmed and soothed me like a crying child being picked up by its mother. A rush of emotion surging through me, I dropped down on my knees and prayed, "God, if this is You talking to me, trying to stop me from doing something bad to those people, if this is You, *forgive me!* Forgive me for everything! Forgive me for all I've done! Help me! Stop me!"

Alone in that hotel room, bathed in tears, I surrendered my life wholeheartedly to God. I spoke out loud and ran off a long list of all of the sins that I could remember, as if doing so was handing them over to Him for forgiveness. At the end of my prayer, I added, "And God, there's a whole lot of other stuff I've done that I can't remember. Please forgive me for that, too." Flooded with relief from the shame, I snatched the bottle of VSOP off the table. To seal my deal with the Almighty, I twisted the top off the VSOP, poured it down the toilet and then threw it in the garbage.

And life began again.

Sticking to God's Script

That was the starting point—or maybe, it was my starting-*over* part. Either way on that day, I committed myself to God, and I committed to being done with liquor at the same time.

I began to picture God in my life, and if God was here, He was going to work things out. I realized I must wholeheartedly look to the Lord to forgive my sins and change the direction of my life—I *was* the lost sheep, the lost coin, and the prodigal son. My crimes didn't stop God from speaking to me, calling me by my name and showing me His divine intention to guide me into His will.

That created an appetite for God in me. And once whetted that appetite created the pursuit of change in me. That appetite drove my attention off the world around me and placed it almost completely on Him. It was as if I exchanged my desire for liquor and all evil, for a driving desire for God. *Who is this God that talks to killers and stops them in their tracks?* I thought.

So, I made a vow to stick with God's script. I caught the first bus back to Seattle. Meeting with my lawyer, I turned myself into the authorities. I walked into the penitentiary with the reputation of being a brutal hoodlum, a criminal thug. I was "Big Art". Most of the inmates knew me: *Big Art, he's a snap artist, he's crazy, he's a rider!* What they didn't know was I no longer identified as "Big Art"—I identified as the man God said I was. And yet the truth is, I didn't know who that man *was*. My violent past, my abusive upbringing, and my environment had molded me and shaped me. My past still spoke to me, darkening my thoughts. *You're a gang-banger. A drug dealer. A stone-cold killer.*

That's who I thought I was. That's how I identified myself. I was chained to that identity—inside; I was still Big Art, the dude with the heavy hands who had done all sorts of wicked and evil things.

At the same time, I was also fighting to be free. Inside, I was someone looking for change. Inside, I believed I could morph into something different. I could become who I was created to be. I could transform from a convict into a con-tributing member of society.

I kept that faith. I believed. And quietly, behind the scenes, my identity was being solidified by God.

Defeating discouragement became my first mission. In the past, I hadn't known my purpose. Thus, my potential remained untapped, and I was forced to experiment. As a result, my life got completely turned upside down—anytime you experiment with something, you risk using it wrong. By experimenting, my true potential was abused, and the path God had plotted for me never unlocked.

Unintentionally or not, I'd made poor decisions and abused my purpose, my true identity. I thought, *My iden-tity brought on adversity!*—by chasing the wrong identity I'd caused so many tragedies, created so much trauma, and was the source of shame and torture for so many others. As I pursued the voice of God, I was reminded of all I had done.

All the people I'd hurt.

All the pain I'd caused.

All the wickedness I'd played a part in.

But because my new identity told me I was someone God wanted, someone God loved, someone God considered valuable, I was prompted again and again to live by my faith.

Repping God

One day, the chaplain entered my wing. His presence seemed heroic, supernatural. Seated in the day room at the tables, he opened to the book of Chronicles and told us the story of Jabez. Jabez was a man who'd sown incredible pain and sorrow in the lives of his family and neighbors—in fact, Jabez's name literally meant "he will cause pain." But, in 1 Chronicles 4:10 (KJV), he begged and pleaded and cried out to God in prayer. *"…Oh that thou wouldest bless me indeed, and enlarge my coast, and that thine hand might be with me, and that thou wouldest keep me from evil, that it may not grieve me!"* Jabez was basically saying, Stop me from causing people pain! My favorite part of that scripture was the resolution: *"…And God granted him that which he requested."*

Huddled in my dark cell, struggling with my identity and who I was, I prayed the prayer of Jabez, hoping it would be granted to me.

Out of curiosity, I began reading my Bible. Even though I'd read through the Bible—once, twice—because now, I was rapidly devouring God's Word. I'd read twenty chapters in a day. My eyes stung from staring at the pages in excitement. My fingertips explored the book's strange terrain. One day, I opened to John 8:31–32 (NKJV) and read:

> *Then Jesus said to those Jews who believed Him, "If you abide in My word, you are My*

disciples indeed. And you shall know the truth, and the truth shall make you free."

Quietly I took that into my spirit. *Okay,* I thought. *If God saw me as valuable enough to speak to me, to intervene in my situation and circumstances to stop me from causing more pain, and if He considered me valuable enough to identify me in Luke, chapter 15, like a lost sheep, a lost coin, and a lost son, then I too, should find who God says I truly am in the Scriptures.*

And I began to look.

Part of my struggle in discovering my identity was being marked as the First Chief of the Black Gangster Disciples. Often as I walked the prison yard or strolled the tiers, someone would shout out, "Di-sci-ples!" Convicts would throw up their gang signs because, by their definition, I represented a nation of gangsters.

But by God's definition, I was now *His* disciple. So, I plugged into His Word and plunged deep into the Scriptures. I said to myself, *If John the Baptist found himself in Isaiah, chapter 11, and Jesus found His identity in Isaiah, Chapter 61, then I too can find my identity in these pages.*

Being a Gangster Disciple, I'd constructed a noose out of my failures. In contrast, as God's disciple, I was filling up with forgiveness, exchanging my rage and violence for a faith-filled life that would keep me free of spiritual toxins, changing minute by minute, hour by hour, day by day.

But was God done with me? No, He wasn't! So, I began studying and studying, striving to be more and more like what I saw in His Word.

With what could be considered fanatic intensity, I studied, mined the Bible for truth, and learned. Every time I learned something or received an expression of His will, I didn't question God. I didn't doubt. I didn't reject.

I just *did it.*

But God didn't let up. He pushed me to keep going. The Spirit of God spoke to me and told me to contact a certain family member. I hadn't seen him since I was five years old. Regardless, God prodded me to reach out to what I thought was this evil man, and ask him to forgive me.

I was horrified. *God, are You serious? This dude owes* me *forgiveness! He's the one who disappeared when I was five! He's the one who was a heroin addict and a liar!*

I was angered and petrified of picking up the phone. The more I resisted, the more God nudged. "Call him, and tell him you forgive him. And ask him to forgive you."

Unprepared for God's request, I relented and phoned him. A stretch of silence followed my shaky introduction. After half a dozen efforts, I remember thinking, *Man, my message isn't getting through.* Holding back my tears, I listened as he told me, "Wow, I can tell you've been spending some time with God!"

Spending some time with God? In a whirl of disbelief, I repeated the phrase in my mind. As I hung up, I felt a gaping hole in my existence suddenly filled. As the puzzle pieces of my life began falling into place, I was reminded that my identity was to be found in God, not in my family, not in the absence of my family, not in the addictions of my family, nor the abuse.

My identity came from God.

I'd never experienced such amazing peace. God's plan had worked the impossible. And now, I wanted to know what He had planned for me.

You Know My Name

I relied upon God's bold words to boost my faith. One day, while locked in my cell, I brooded on the question of my new identity. I spoke to God about the thug I had once been, and all God had done to rescue me. With sudden clarity, I realized I needed one thing more.

God, I prayed, *You gave Simon another name and called him Peter. You gave Abram another name and called him Abraham. Perhaps You can give me another name that would identify what it is You're planning for me.* In a flash, God took me back to the original scripture John 8:31–32 (NASB): *"If you continue in My word then you are truly disciples of Mine; and you will know the truth, and the truth will make you free."* He said to start introducing myself as Free Man.

"Lord," I said, "this sounds crazy! You want me to introduce myself as a free man while I'm incarcerated amongst killers?"

And the Lord simply answered, *"Yep."*

So, I began introducing myself as Free Man. I had come to the conclusion that I am who God says I am, regardless of where I am, who people think I am, and even regardless of how I feel.

I am who God says I am.

And the transformation began.

I won't say it happened overnight. It didn't. But my commitment to the pursuit of God was air-tight. God's promise says, *Jesus purchased you. Jesus redeemed you. You are forgiven. You are loved. And there's nothing you can do to earn a higher status with Me.*

That's what God was trying to get across. I was broken; God restores broken people. The struggle of my identity that brought on adversity was necessary for my change, as I began to morph from one man into another.

And yet, I still needed something more.

It took some time before I knew what it was.

My Secret Place

During my pursuit of change, one particular story from the Word of God stood out. That was the story of the seed.

The Bible often speaks about the Kingdom of God being like a man sowing a seed. Jesus is called *the seed*; the Word of God is called *the seed*. I was amazed when I recognized this. I realized that anytime something requires change, it must first go into a secluded place, a dark place, a hidden place, like a seed buried deep underground. The seed goes into the earth, and once it's sown, it begins the journey of breaking through, springing up, and sprouting.

This electrified me. *Even though not everyone can see I'm changed, even though I'm still Big Art to these cats in here, even though I still struggle with thoughts of putting hands on guys in anger, even though my family doesn't trust my talking about Jesus is real, and even though I'm dealing with all this heavy stuff, I feel as if my life is a seed. One I have given to God and watched Him sow it into a secret place so that it can begin to develop and grow.*

Even though my transformation was hidden to some, I knew the Word of God was working. My seed wouldn't return void. It had to prosper.

As time passed, I slowly noticed a change. I began speaking differently. *Corny,* I would have called it back in the day because I was so used to being aggressive and hostile with my language and my threatening tone of voice.

My thoughts and behavior also changed. I'd think, *I would have slapped that dude back in the day, but now I'm forgiving and kind.* I'm not suggesting that I became a poster child for good manners, but observing this phenomenon, I was convinced it was God at work, morphing "Big Art" into the man I was meant to be.

As the old "Art" faded, God showed me His power is bigger than my past. God's intervention in my life was now undeniable. Although, I knew I could expect opposition and persecution from boldly obeying God.

What I needed was a safe location, a secret place, for my final morphing. Clark Kent ducked into a phone booth when he transformed into Superman. Bruce Banner hid himself away so that he could morph into the Incredible Hulk. Even a tiny creature such as the caterpillar spins itself a cocoon—a hidden chamber where it transforms into a moth or butterfly.

Like them, I needed to be somewhere far away, secluded from the negative lies spinning around in my mind, where I could hear God's voice above all others, and allow God the opportunity to work on me and change me. I needed to embrace that season of change, and allow God's Holy Spirit to transform me, to do impossible things for God's Kingdom.

To be morphed into the real me, I'd need to pursue God in my secret place.

Chapter Three

The Secret Place

Pursuing God makes you a weapon. You're engaged in warfare, fighting for your destiny, taking back turf from Satan. You're called up from the dust to be a warrior on His battleground—and that battle can create chaos in your life.

In prison, I couldn't escape the chaos. One of the most powerful things I learned, as I grew and transitioned from hood-thinking into good-thinking, was how private practice created public power. As I studied the Bible, digging deeper and deeper, I ran across a scripture in Matthew 6:6 (NKJV), which revealed a hidden paradox.

> *But you, when you pray, go into your room,*
> *and when you have shut the door, pray to*
> *your Father, who is in the secret place; and*
> *your Father, who sees in secret, will reward*
> *you openly.*

This verse in Matthew stunned me. It returned me, in my childlike faith, to my belief in superheroes, how Clark Kent snuck into phone booths and morphed into something spectacular, something supernatural, a deliverer and rescuer. I felt that God was prompting me, giving me the opportunity to seek out and find my own quiet, hidden-away place.

My private place.

My superpower accessing secret place.

A place that was far away from everybody, where I could be transformed.

Matthew 6:6 explained something to me. God yearned to bless me. He wanted me to discover that secret place. And then go into that place and change.

Triggering My Destiny

That powerful verse in Matthew also blessed me for another reason. It showed me that God *sees* in secret, yet *rewards* us openly. He promises that our secret mindsets, our private beliefs, our unshakeable faith, and the faith-filled life-styles we practice when we're alone will eventually bear fruit, which will be seen and made evident to everyone.

Luke 8:17 (KJV), gave me another one of God's proclamations:

> *For nothing is secret, that shall not be made manifest; neither anything hid, that shall not be known or come abroad.*

That's revolutionary! All things that are hidden will eventually come out. Luke 8:17 strengthened my inner resilience. I saw the possibility of my victory rising up from the secret place allowing God to deliver me from oppressive bondage. Certainly, being incarcerated helped me understand that.

To God, sin is sin, whether it's hidden in darkness or manifested in the light of day.

However, my dilemma was complicated. How, locked away from society, could I create hidden times and meeting places with God? If I was to be rescued by the Master's hand, lifted from sinking down into old bad habits and criminal behaviors, how would I begin that upward journey?

Here's how it happened.

Every morning, after breakfast, when I was still in my cell, I committed to doing 500 pushups while reading a chapter from the Bible between each set. I would do fifty pushups, read a chapter; do fifty more pushups, read a chapter; do fifty more pushups, and read a chapter. Each day, I'd end up reading ten chapters at a minimum. I also spent time in my cell asking God questions about the stuff I learned.

This sounds easier to believe than it was to practice. Still, I had childlike faith, to the degree that I didn't just race through the Bible like I was trying to get to *The End*. I saturated myself with God's Word. I challenged myself to wake from my lulled state of disconnection. I committed to erasing my foundation of fear, doubt, self-destruction, and negativity.

I wasn't a great prayer warrior. I'd been a thief and a habitual liar. I'd been living a life of hypocrisy. Now I was fighting for my life—but somehow, I knew that the answers to everything could be found inside the pages of my Bible.

One day, I discovered a scripture in Psalms 91:1 (NKJV):

He who dwells in the secret place of The
Most High Shall abide under the shadow
of the Almighty.

As I read that, the darkness behind my eyelids filled with bright light. I realized: *God will be with me, in my secret place, my hidden place—protecting me, communicating with me, helping me, and teaching me.* As a matter of fact, the Psalms 91:1 verse made me think about an eagle—the shadow in Psalms represented how the father eagle protects their baby chicks in the nest, in the secret place, in the shadow of the father. That's how I pictured it.

That eye-opening moment flipped a switch in my destiny. More and more, I spent time alone with God. Before I went to sleep in my cell, I would pray and ask God what book I should read next—there were many Christian books available, yet not all contained the kind of soul-winning content that could stir an ex-gangster. "God, should I read this one?" I'd innocently ask, and God would say, "Yes, you can read that Charles Capps book. But don't read the book by that other author."

God knew whose word I needed to hear. Foundationally, He was leading me down a pathway, out of the pit and the prison, toward a quality of character that would produce a complete change. He was teaching me to lean in, listen closely, encouraging me, feeding me, and feeding my desire for a new identity—one that could endure the pain I'd faced before achieving my dreams that wasn't afraid to leave behind my cage of comfort and take bold risks.

He blessed me with different times and places in the day that I would call triggers. In the shower, I would pray in the spirit and ask God questions. In the yard, I would quote scriptures I wanted to memorize after each lap before I climbed on the dip or pull-up bar. Before I slept, I'd read from the book God suggested, then drop into a deep and peaceful sleep talking to God, asking questions about the book.

Looking to the Lord for guidance began to shape me. He uncovered the hidden questions in my heart. When I read the scripture about Joseph, how his brothers threw him into a pit and placed him into slavery, yet later on, Joseph forgave those very same brothers, I was perplexed. I craved understanding. I asked God, "How is it possible to go through all that pain and suffering, deal with all those struggles and trials as a result of your own brothers hating you, and *not hate them back?*"

Running to God for answers, I persevered. "How is that so?" I whispered to God. I'd be thinking about Joseph's story the rest of the day, shaking my head. "Lord, that's *impossible!* How do you forgive people like that? They put Joseph in a pit and sold him as a slave. How do you forgive people for that level of hate?"

I'd wait. And wait. Suddenly, out of nowhere, God's answer would come. Might be a day later. Might be a week. And yet always, He'd set in motion the wheels of my understanding. God would nudge me to read Kenneth Copeland's magazines, Jesse Duplantis' articles, or Joyce Meyer's books. And while I was reading a book, I'd flip to a chapter on forgiveness, and *boom!*—it would give me the answer to the question I'd asked about Joseph in my secret place.

Something about the way the answers came made my secret place more precious. It made my intimate time, my alone time with God, more powerful, more profitable, and more valuable. In my secret place, negative thoughts didn't bombard my mind. Time froze. In that place where nobody but God was watching, where the people out on the yard were screaming and hollering about Big Art and the brutal things he'd done and the craziness he'd created, I could get alone with God and ask questions.

And receive answers.

God's answers magnified the secret place. Thus, my appetite for God became an appetite for intimacy. My secret place lifted, encouraged, and shaped me. There, my thought-life became transformed from natural to supernatural. I learned God could love even a lifelong thug and criminal like me, a man who'd dipped down into the deepest depths of destructive behavior. I learned how the love of God not only pursued me and spoke to me and nurtured me—it challenged me to change every detail in my life.

God dared me. *Dream. Then dream again. And reach for those dreams.*

The Dreaming Place

I had stopped dreaming. Prisoners in lock-up don't have much reason to dream. But now, God gave me the extraordinary boldness to dream again, to take the stories I'd been told in my secret place and put myself in the picture.

Mark, chapter 5, showed me the story of Jairus, who begs Jesus to heal his sick daughter. Look at the story from the viewpoint of Jairus. I'm Jairus, with a sick child in need of healing, desperate because time is running out and I've tried everything—I've spent all my money, traveled great distances, moaned feverish prayers, yet nothing has healed her. Then I hear about this man named Jesus, who's going about healing people. In desperation, I seek Him out, prowling after Him in the crowded streets. I push through the crowd and finally get to Jesus, and I desperately beg Him, "Jesus, my daughter is sick, come!" And Jesus, without thinking about it, says, "I will go with you."

"Come lay your hands on her, and she will be healed!" I plead. And Jesus says, "I will go with you."

Talk about a powerful moment! Now we're heading in the direction of my child. Jesus has promised to heal her! As we're moving through the crowd, and I'm elbowing and jostling people back, out of nowhere this woman pushes through, shoves her way up to Jesus, and *touches Him…*

and all of a sudden, Jesus *stops*. "Why are we stopping?" I plead, my desperation out of control. "I want to see my child healed!" But Jesus stops because this woman had *touched Him*, and pulled power out of Him, without Jesus's knowing it. And while I'm watching this through the eyes of Jairus, and hearing what the woman proclaims took place in her, the miracle she experienced that she's been freed from suffering just from touching Jesus's hem. It builds my belief, my faith, my confidence—this man truly is the Savior, the man who can heal my little daughter!

Then I climb out of the eyes of Jairus, and into the eyes of the woman. She's experienced an issue of blood for twelve years, seen many physicians, without being healed. Closing my eyes, I see inside her failing body, her broken heart, her wounded soul. Then witnessing the arrival of Jesus, hope explodes out of her. Pressing forward, with steadfast determination, she pushes, shoulders, and shoves through the crowd to reach this man. As I dream through her eyes, the risk she's taking is overwhelming—she's praying this stranger can do something for her, can cure her, can heal her pain.

Blindly setting aside her fears I see her reach out, her fingers quivering, straining for the hem of His garment. Not intimidated—instead, believing what people say about Jesus will happen. I see the garment touched. I see the crowd around her hushed, frightened. I see through the eyes of the disciples who were attempting to protect the Messiah as He walked through town. Eventually, I get to the place where I can see through the eyes of Jesus.

Now, I challenge you to put yourself in my place. I was a mess. I was a thief, a robber, a hustler, and a banger—a deadly, destructive individual who had his life intervened in by a living, loving God. And I was wrestling with this moment because God wanted me to see things through His Son's eyes.

His Way.

Fortunately, God persuades me. In the dream, I climb into the eyes of Jesus, into the eyes of the Messiah. I see myself fulfilling my great purpose, walking in the direction of a house in the town where a man's daughter will be healed.

As I'm walking, I picture myself as Jesus and feel His power. As the hem of my garment is touched, I feel the power surging out of me. ("Virtue is gone out of me," is what Jesus actually said (Luke 8:46, KJV). As Jesus, I see tears spilling out of this woman's grateful eyes. This woman has *faith!*— She's pressed forward, without fear or doubt, to receive healing from the almighty power of God. She's taken a chance, a risk, a leap of faith, and now is renewed. Having received Jesus's power, she can walk in the newness of life. All this I saw and felt, in my secret place.

The road I traveled to transformation was a rough and rocky one. All along the path, God needed to persuade me to keep coming back to Him. I kept questioning myself: *What's God's plan here? What was I doing in a secret place?*

I was escaping bondage.

I was overcoming oppression.

I was dreaming.

What was I doing in the secret place? I was asking God questions and receiving bold answers.

What was I doing in the secret place? I was growing from a baby into a boy, and from a boy into a man of God.

Exposing My Secrets

In my room, in my secret place, God revealed something else to me. He exposed the conflicts and inconsistencies I was experiencing with His Word. For instance, after reading a story in the Bible, I'd find myself deeply disturbed and troubled that I wasn't able to think like the characters in Matthew, Acts, or Romans. I didn't believe like these men. I didn't behave like these men. And I didn't see results—I tended to return to my old defaults.

Troubled by this, I questioned God. I prayed God would reveal and seal His truth deep within my heart. By embracing my true identity, He exposed the false belief systems I had been taught, and the patterns that were created in my life causing me to fail again and again.

At the same time, the word "cycle" came up while I was in the secret place. The Lord began to show me how cycles were born in my life, how those cycles created beliefs, which had become strongholds in my life. I believed if you were against me, you were my enemy. If you were my enemy, my opposition, I was determined to rid myself of you or your influence. And I had many weapons to achieve this.

I believed fear was a weapon. Fear was a tool of warfare. Violence could bring about any desired result. Pain and suffering could manipulate any situation. I believed all sorts of manipulative and destructive principles. Each of these was exposed in me as I began to dream, meditate, and sit in the secret place and ask God, "*Why did I think that?*"

One thing you'll learn from God in the secret place, He'll not only tell you *His* secrets, He will also help you overcome the pain of having exposed you to *your* secrets.

God Flips the Script

In the secret place, God exposed to me who I really was. What I really believed. What caused me to fall back on certain destructive behaviors. And why I continued in those behaviors.

One time in my bunk, I was extremely mad at my wife because she'd promised to send me some pictures of a family party. Those pictures never arrived. Enraged at my wife, I thought to myself, *She's the enemy. She's against me. She doesn't understand the pain and suffering I'm going through.*

So, I climbed under the covers and thought to myself that my cellmate would be wise not to mess with me today, don't say anything because I might flip out and do something that we'd both regret. My anger was looking for an outlet.

That's when I heard God reach out to me in my secret place. "Why are you so mad?" He asked. I grumbled, "Because my wife said she was going to send those pictures, and she didn't. She lied. She doesn't understand that in prison, the only way I can see freedom is if she takes a picture of it, puts it in an envelope, and mails it to me. It's not just a package of pictures—it's a portrait of *freedom.* And if she doesn't mail me a picture, then I never get to see freedom. All I see are these four cell walls and these cold concrete hallways and this prison surrounded by a barbed-wire fence, which reminds me I'm in bondage because of my bad decisions. And I don't get to experience freedom until she sends me the pictures!"

A moment passed. I felt my heart hammering, my head ready to explode. Finally, I heard the peaceful voice of God. "Is that *really* why you're mad?" At that moment, a memory exploded in my mind, as real as any Hollywood movie. Digging into a memory deeply rooted in my soul, God showed me how I could flip the script of my past.

I began to envision myself as a child. I watched myself getting a call from my mom during the holidays, telling me a certain relative was on the phone from California. I watched the child-me rush to the phone to speak with him, a heroin addict who had disappeared when I was five years old.

I saw myself asking, "When are you going to come see me?"

The words leaped out of the phone. "I'll be there soon," he'd say.

I threw the phone down and bolted off, elated. But in my heart, I knew he had lied to me. He said the same thing year after year but never showed up. Sadly, I never saw him. I didn't know what he looked like. I hadn't seen him in years. Almost as if he didn't consider me valuable enough to come and see me, didn't love me enough to make his words come to pass.

And because I felt less and less valuable, I grew angrier and angrier. I thought to myself that those who say they love you can easily discard of you when distances are involved. It made me feel like I wanted to distance myself from the people who will disappoint me more and more.

Meanwhile, back in my bunk, in my secret place, I'm talking to God, angrily voicing my feelings, telling God how mad I am at my wife because she didn't send me the pictures she promised. The Master's hand then revealed itself. God showed me the truth; I'm not mad at my wife. I'm mad at a *precedent;* the first thing I ever experienced pertaining to that issue. In the legal system, once a rule or law has been established, it creates a precedent. This rule or law can then be used by the court or other judicial bodies when deciding later cases with similar issues.

According to the Lord, a precedent had been established by my family. Because someone I loved promised something, and their words never came to pass, it caused me to feel like I wasn't valuable—to the point that my hurt as a child became violent rage as a young man. Because of my upbringing, I'd become a vengeful adult with a little boy trapped inside, still raging at the people I love when they promise something, and it doesn't come true. Their failure makes me feel unworthy, unloved. As a result, I set myself on a downward path, dodging and ducking God's path for my life, doing everything within my power to get away from the real me.

Even worse, my downward path made me want to get away from *Him.*

Handing over Yesterday for Tomorrow

That day in the secret place was the beginning of my journey. That day, I unlocked the pain I still experienced as a twenty-seven-year-old man. My rebellion had caused me to suffer consequences. In that powerful moment, I saw just how misguided I'd become.

"Okay," I said to myself, the battle for my soul beginning, "so that's what it is. I'm mad at my wife just like I'm mad at those closest to me who said they would do things and didn't follow through. And I'm mad at all the people I've ever loved, and everybody I thought loved me. I never believed it was real love because they would make promises that never came true. I'm still throwing down vengeance on all of them."

What God revealed to me next startled me. He showed me I had to forgive the person who'd established that first precedent in my spirit. Otherwise, the past is holding me hostage. I am declaring I'm worthless. I'm not valuable enough for anybody to love me, to show me compassion, to genuinely follow through with the promises they make. All that came out of one deep moment with God, in the secret place.

Much more would be necessary for me to unpack and purge the excruciating pain of who I'd become. However, as I unlocked the pain, as I broke through my resistance, I became more compelled to speak God's promises over my life boldly, and more committed to talking to God about my secrets. Even though the answers didn't always come directly from God—sometimes it was from a magazine, a chapter of the Bible, or something I saw or heard at a Christian service or even in a song—I knew it was God speaking to my spirit.

That process changed me. It restructured me. Taking that first bold step magnified the value of the secret place.

My devotion time with God became mandatory. God promised if I met Him, in the secret place, victory would come, one small step, one small decision at a time. God's amazing power would be manifested. Things, which had bound and chained me could be overcome, and my destiny would be unlocked by His supernatural love showing me how to untangle every knot in my train of thought.

My commitment to change helped me die to my old self. God's mercy created my newfound character in the secret place. Though I didn't know a kingdom warrior was being created, I drank from His cup of mercy gratefully.

Following that conversation with God, I forgave everyone—my family and my wife. God persuaded me to stop struggling and stumbling. He wanted me to live the life *He'd* promised. Forgiving helped me stop judging tomorrow by yesterday. Forgiving made me see how yesterday played a part in what I thought today, which played a part in how I thought tomorrow—unless, that is, I was willing to hand over my yesterday for God's tomorrow.

That's the miracle God wrought. Not by lightning bolts or thunder. But by my choice to wholeheartedly seek Him.

I gave Him my yesterdays. He gave me His tomorrow.

Don't get me wrong, giving Him my yesterdays was painful. It reopened wounds and pains of the past. And yet, sacrificing my past allowed Him to heal me. As a result, my practice of pursuing God in the secret place gave birth to a public power, which manifested itself in a spiritual house-cleaning, a new version of Art, a man empowered with new principles, new thought patterns, new behaviors.

Sometimes I'd come out of the secret place, and eight or nine hours had ticked by. To me, it seemed crazy! How could that much time fly by? But time was no longer important—pushing through the trials and tribulations of change was now my learning journey.

The pain was being exposed. Problems revealed. Precedents of negative thoughts released and cycles that created past behaviors broken, all by the mighty love of God and the glorious Word of God. Forgiveness was being forged, enabling me to break free from my former thug life, the freeze-frame of disobedience I'd been stuck, bound, and chained in.

I was morphing from a shady, shifty, and miserable man into a man of joy and abundant hope. Each day was a new start, a new opportunity to change. I had no power to manufacture that change. I needed God's power to change if the change was to be lasting. I found that power in His Word.

Battling the Riptide of Wickedness

This miraculous healing of my wounded spirit brewed all kinds of internal conflicts. Being "Big Art," gangster disciple from the Central District of Seattle, I still retained negative thought patterns that caused me to stumble. The temptation to fall back, to surrender to my negative beliefs, was a battle to be fought every day. Moment by moment, I tapped into my new warrior's heart, the holy resurrection power that connected me to God in the face of adversity.

When I called my wife back, after hanging up because the pictures she'd promised hadn't arrived, I apologized, explaining I'd had a talk with God. God showed me she wasn't doing anything to hurt me; she just didn't understand the significance of those pictures, which symbolized freedom in the midst of bondage. As I asked her to forgive me, a strange thing happened...

Part of the "old Art" reappeared, judging me for my weakness, calling me a "sucker," a "punk".

It was a battle for my very soul. The old part of me rejected my hard-fought liberation from the negative noise, refusing to accept the new, changed me. It yearned to shut down my spiritual wake-up call, my siren of hope, to drag me back to the pit, to the riptide of wickedness that had always sucked me down.

My downward lifestyle was still calling me. I couldn't escape the negative thoughts floating around in my mind. Dark chapters from my life resurfaced. Worst of all, the call from God felt like a betrayal.

I needed a defense against that negative call, one higher than the walls of Jericho. But where would I find that, in a house of corrections? How would I conquer my negative chatter? How would I battle my internal struggles, with nothing but fear, shame, condemnation, and discouragement surrounding me? And if I couldn't emerge victorious from my internal rejection, how would I defeat the world's external rejection?

CHAPTER FOUR

THE REJECTION CONNECTION

One day, sitting alone on my bunk, my pillow pressed against my ears to keep out the murderous screams and howls of my fellow inmates, I experienced my own personal revelation, my thunder-and-lightning flash of insight. Call it my own Moses and the burning-bush moment.

That day, I had a long talk in my spirit with God about how I was judging myself. Self-condemnation was an unquestionable reality in the life of a prisoner in lock-up. My mind couldn't lay down my old sinful life on the altar of God's unobstructed love. I'd find myself alone on my bunk, looking at my past, the things I'd said and done, and hating who I was. It was as if my biggest battle was me struggling with me, with who I was, while I was working on receiving who I wanted to be.

Locked in a cage, without freedom, I struggled mightily to make that transition. I worked on it. And waited. Nevertheless, waiting only made me feel helpless. In-between waiting for this transition, I would see myself making right decisions and doing the right thing, then turning right around and making wrong decisions and doing wrong. I remained stuck in my old default settings. While I admired and felt energized by the new Art, I felt growing inside; I couldn't build on it. Mistake after painful mistake followed.

As I sat listening to a teaching on a Romans scripture one day, it hit me that God was clearly revealing something. I questioned God, "Lord, show me what is taking place inside of me. Help me understand what's going on, so I don't give up in the midst of my struggle because it seems like I fail too much."

I could feel myself almost panic, breathing deeply in and out, waiting for the answer. That's when God planted in my heart the verse from Ephesians 4:22–24 (NKJV),

> *That you put off, concerning your former conduct, the old man which grows corrupt according to the deceitful lusts, and be renewed in the spirit of your mind, and that you put on the new man which was created according to God, in true righteousness and holiness.*

My mind was racing. *Wait, hold up, what are you saying?* In that instant, I asked, God showed me with crystal-clarity the meaning of this amazing scripture. It's meaning is *transition.*

During transition, a man is equal to the caterpillar inside its cocoon; struggling to morph, and to change. Something old must be taken off before something new can be put on.

Meditating on this settled my heart. I saw that in certain areas in my life I was putting something new on top, while I allowed the "old man" to remain alive underneath.

I questioned God about this. "*How can I put off the struggles going on inside of me because of my old beliefs recreat-*

ing old behaviors? And why were the new behaviors struggling to take root?"

That's when God opened my spirit and showed me the Law of Displacement through the teachings of Jerry Savelle on a Kenneth Copeland, Trinity Broadcasting Network television show.

The Law of Displacement says if I have a cup and it's full of coffee, and I pour a big pitcher of milk into the cup, the coffee will remain black at the top because the milk only penetrates the surface. The milk then sinks to the bottom and begins to saturate and take up residence in the cup. The milk displaces the black coffee. With the same force that's poured into the cup, the milk forces out what was already inside. As it's penetrated, the coffee turns light cream-colored; yet as the overflow continues, the whole cup will be slowly transformed until everything in the cup is turned milk-white.

Like the cup, I recognized that my life was similar. This set the wheels in my brain in motion. I understood that it was the Law of Displacement taking place in my spirit. But, coming to this dramatic conclusion only filled me with more puzzling questions. I asked God, "What is it that's pouring into me that is bringing the change? What is the old me being replaced with?" Within seconds, the answer popped into my head. Then, of course, I thought, *it's Your Word.*

That second burning-bush moment provoked my attention. Naturally, I began to second-guess it. I knew ignoring God's Word wouldn't produce transformation. Additionally, the Word of God came into me in many different profound ways. I was reading the Bible out loud. I was praying along with asking questions. I confessed my sins to God as soon as I recognized them. Somehow, I still felt I was missing out on activating my transformation, that greater purpose resident within me from God.

One day, as I was watching a Benny Hinn TV show, I witnessed God performing the impossible, the supernatural; a nine-year-old girl who'd been born blind miraculously received her sight. This overwhelmed me. I sat in awestruck silence, my eyes glued to the TV screen, while in the midst of the studio audience shouting hallelujahs and going wild this young girl opened her eyes and miraculously *saw*, oblivious to the crazy noise going on around her. For the very first time, her brain was taking in this new information—light, color, movement. She was almost frozen in a slow-moving stare. What swamped my mind the most was the girl's father—in the instant his daughter received sight, he dropped to the ground, weeping, crying, and wailing. He was overwhelmed at the thought that his daughter, born blind, could now see.

As I sat there that day, tears welling up in my eyes, I praised God for healing that little girl. I worshiped Him and thanked Him and lifted my hands to Him. It was as if I couldn't thank Him enough. And at that moment, amazed at the life-altering gift God had planted inside this little girl, I engaged myself in a new gift, breaking out into prayer in what the Bible calls *tongues*.

Speaking in Tongues

Speaking in tongues is a holy gift—a divinely granted tool identified by glorious, unintelligible speech. For believers who are filled with the Holy Spirit, speaking in tongues is used to build our most holy faith and magnify God.

The moment I broke into tongues, everything in my life changed. At first, I was amazed, and my mind filled with questions. *What is this? Another warped way to humiliate myself with God?* Then came a breakthrough moment of clarity. According to my Bible studies, I'd been filled with a divine baptism of the Holy Spirit—yet silently, I second-guessed this and debated what had really taken place. Ultimately, I learned to process this new voice. And I learned to use this mighty spiritual weapon.

I prayed in tongues; I worshiped in tongues; I read the Bible while praying in tongues; I thanked God in tongues for His divine miracle with the little blind girl. As bizarre as it felt, I found speaking in tongues reversed the devil's stranglehold on my heart and my soul. It seemed that almost immediately after I received the baptism of the Holy Spirit my understanding of the Scriptures multiplied a thousand times.

My training grew sharper, my walk with God intensified, His voice piercing through the roar of doubts in my mind. Reading more and more books by one of my favorite authors, Charles Capps, I became educated on the importance of the words of my mouth. I began to confess God's Truth, God's Word, what God said about me, to imagine what purpose God had planned for me.

More and more words from the Spirit poured into my cup. As they poured into my cup, they caused things to surface that I didn't know were there.

This insight ripped the lid off my old sins. Although I thought the "old man" was dead inside me, his beliefs, his behaviors, and his wicked mindsets still lurked, still remained. That stuff continued vomiting to the surface—the violence, the brutality, the hostility, the aggression. God's love brought all that to the surface as the Word of God was poured into me.

And I struggled. In my displacement, I failed, and I fell.

Incident after incident, I'd walk in integrity, my loving words matching my actions. Then I'd turn around in a fit of anger because I'd lost a chess game to another inmate and threaten to rag doll him in the dayroom. Trapped on the outside and sometimes feeling miserable on the inside,

I had more question marks than exclamation points in my transformation.

What has God showed me? I wondered. His answer transformed my unspeakable anguish into something He could use.

Displacement. He explained displacement was taking place. Even though my old sin was being exposed and surfacing, God encouraged me not to grow weary in doing well because it was His proof I was changing.

Change seemed impossible. On the inside, I rejected myself. Evil thoughts rejected good thoughts. The good thoughts rejected evil thoughts. Even the transformative love of God wrestled with me. It was like being locked in a dark room for a long period of time. As your eyes transition to the darkness, the pupils dilate so that they can receive as much light as possible. But the moment you flip on the lights, your eyes squint in pain. So, you close your eyes as you attempt to push back against the light that is entering too rapidly.

The pressure of the Word going into me was bringing painful change. I was dealing with anguish and discomfort from transitioning. From within my spirit, I rejected these old thoughts, ideas, behaviors, and beliefs that threatened to destroy my newfound purpose. Every time God showed another deficiency in my life, simultaneously he offered up an invitation to fill that void with His grace.

The Rejection Connection

As I humbled myself before the Spirit of God, His Word stirred up a platform, a stage for His divine teaching, which I devoured with unshakable confidence. Prompted by His Word, a new concept streamed through my mind—the rejection connection. I began to see how rejection in me, as well as rejection from others, affected me.

No man or woman was created to be rejected. All of us were created to be accepted and loved. But when sin entered the world in the Garden of Eden, man chose to reject God by rejecting God's Word. And in so doing, mankind sowed the seeds of rejection for all eternity, which unlocked rejection all over the earth.

Look at the story of Cain and Abel. Both brought offerings to God—yet one brought an offering that was accepted, and the other brought an offering that was rejected. Like Cain, I, too, had experienced rejection. And it was that rejection connection that was eating me alive.

In the past, I'd faced little rejection of peers. Everywhere I went, people liked me. I made friends easily, and could hang with any person, any race, any color, any creed. Any room I walked into, I was accepted. I always got the pretty girl. That was the life I knew.

But now, rejection terrified me. Rejection and abandonment played a big part in my fears. It created an orphan's heart—a heart that believed I was unworthy of real love, acceptance, commitment. I'm unworthy of someone staying or sticking by my side. I'm not worthy enough for someone to sacrifice for me. Those abandonment issues created a defense mechanism; my pretend personality. Thus, deep inside, I yearned to be well received and not experience rejection.

As I began to talk to God about the rejection connection, I asked Him, "Lord, has rejection been steering my life? In what areas?" God showed me my sorrow, the pain of being despised and rejected had created a mentality that craves acceptance, that screams, *I will do whatever is necessary to be accepted. I will do whatever is necessary to be someone who's rejection-proof.*

These behaviors fed into my fear of God. I feared God abandoning me over something I'd done because as a child,

I believed something I'd done had caused a particular family member to abandon me. That rejection connection, that fear of abandonment boiling on the inside of me, was screaming louder and louder each day, not only from my fear of God did I suffer, I also suffered from the rejection of myself in the struggles of change.

His Approval Rating

The feelings of being neglected and rejected had formed my orphan's heart. An orphan feels they need to earn love. An orphan doesn't accept love for free. Love needs to be earned, then hoarded and hidden. Anything that comes for free or seems worthless or invaluable, the orphan chooses to reject.

As I began reflecting on my orphan heart, I saw how it drove me in my relationships—even in my relationship with God. I needed to earn God's love, God's commitment, and a position amongst the body of Christ. And what did God do? God showed me there was nothing I could do to earn it! God showed me I could never be rejected by Him. As long as I accepted Him, I was accepted *in* Him.

With God, there's no rejection—only connection and commitment. God commits to taking my sin, and I've committed to receiving what Jesus did for me.

The more God poured His mighty Word into me, the more it washed away my battles with rejection. God's Word sent me running everywhere to uncover the truth. As I learned more and more, I began to ask God, "What other areas am I struggling in? And *why* am I struggling? Is it because Your Word in that area has been rejected? What really is taking place?"

Seeing I still felt disqualified, discontent, and discouraged, God showered me with messages of approval. He broke down my resistance to feeling accepted. He healed me. He renewed me. He revealed His intimate love for me—even while knowing the worst parts of me. His almighty love made me feel worthy.

Even now, I tear up at the memory of that moment of affirmation. So, I began to surrender. I just started surrendering everything to Him.

I said, "Lord, every area where I've rejected Your wisdom, every area where I've rejected Your way of doing things, every area where I've feared things aren't going to work out, and where I've feared abandonment, I surrender to You. I choose now to *refuse*. I *refuse* the fear of rejection. Instead, I commit to turning these things over to You. I surrender to receive freely what You choose to bless me with. Because I can't earn it."

As I began to put down the orphan's heart, I picked up a son's heart. The abandonment issues of my past, the rejection I'd felt, all the struggles I'd gone through as a result of fearing rejection, and all of that vanished. No longer did I fear God would abandon me. I no longer feared my transformation would fail. Instead, I committed freely to accepting what God said and to receive what God had for me in every area of my life.

The Root

At the root of all my abandonment issues, my fears of rejection, my struggle to change was what the old me believed. God prompted me to believe in His promises. And His promises say... *Things change. People change. But God doesn't change.* Instead, God gives us new definitions.

I'd made wrong turns because I followed the wrong definitions, the wrong plans. Now I had an extraordinary opportunity before me. My life, identity, and potential could be redefined by their Author.

Like eyes opening for the first time, I could finally see this. And looking through a new lens of hope and righteousness, no longer blinded or in the grip of my old oppressive mindset, I was now prepared to take the next bold step and apply new definitions to everything I'd ever been taught.

CHAPTER FIVE

• • • • • • •

NEW DEFINITIONS

After getting out of prison, the world seemed different. Coming home was a shock to my system. So much of my old neighborhood, old friends, even my family members had changed while I'd been away. I felt a gap, a deep imbalance, which sent alarm bells screaming in my head.

Being in prison had robbed me of so much. The thing I missed most was freedom—even the simplest freedoms, like choosing what to eat, taking a stroll through the neighborhood, or driving a car. I craved exercising my new freedom. The first thing I did, upon my release, was restore my driver's license. Getting behind the wheel again was a rush, a blast of pure adrenaline. Joy filled my eyes. In that moment, I felt like I'd been given the keys to the whole country.

But I still needed guidance; I still had things to learn. One day, as I was driving with my wife on the freeway, she turned and said to me, "Drive the speed limit." I glanced at my speedometer. I was doing 55 mph, the legal limit. Seeing this, I continued motoring down the freeway. Minutes later, my wife nudged me and said the same thing, "Drive the speed limit." "I *am*," I said, annoyed. I checked the speedometer. I was still clocking in at 55 mph. That's when she told me the speed limit had been changed to 70 mph. Because the legal speed limit had been redefined, I had to make new adjustments in my mindset.

That day was my spiritual wake-up call to the importance of definitions. Because I'd been in prison for over a decade, my definition of the speed limit was locked at 55 mph. Naturally, when I got home and hopped on the freeway, I drove 55 mph. I failed to pay attention to the road signs. I failed to pay attention to the other drivers around me. I simply drove 55 mph and thought I was doing the right thing.

Attention to definitions is crucial. Because as we grow into God's plan for us, definitions change.

Old definitions can be a comfort zone—a safe zone.

New definitions require renewed thinking.

Definitions are the beliefs that determine our behaviors. The way we define things, and what we believe about those definitions, steers our behavior just like I was wrongheadedly steering that car down the freeway.

God's Definition

That point was illustrated to me one day as I was reading Matthew, chapter 16. In Verses 13–17 (KJV), the Book of Matthew says:

> *When Jesus came into the coasts of Caesarea Philippi, he asked his disciples, saying, Whom do men say that I the Son of man am? And they said, Some say that thou art John the Baptist: some, Elias; and others, Jeremiah, or one of the prophets. He saith unto them, But whom say ye that I am?*

And Simon Peter answered and said, Thou art the Christ, the Son of the living God. And Jesus answered and said unto him, Blessed art thou, Simon Barjona: for flesh and blood hath not revealed it unto thee, but my Father which is in heaven.

When I finished reading that verse, I found myself shaking. That story showed me something. The people had a definition of who they believed Jesus was; Peter had a different definition of Jesus. The reason the people's definition was wrong was that they received their definition from their minds, their ignorant ways of thinking. Peter's definition was right because he received his definition straight from God.

Meditating on that scripture, and the beautiful simplicity of the Word of God, I walked away stunned by my newfound understanding of definitions. *The way I'd defined things in the past could have been wrong-minded,* I realized. Sparked by this revelation, I threw away all my old definitions and scrambled to find a new set of definitions for my life. New definitions brought freedom. Knowing God's truth brought liberation.

Having said that my auto-response was to fear these new definitions. But like unknowingly driving the wrong speed, I soon realized I might be doing something completely wrong because my definition is inaccurate, it's not in line with God's definition, with His written Word.

Shortly after gaining that revelation, I was locked in a conversation with someone about the concept of love. As I expressed my love for music, all I heard on the inside was, "*Is that where I told you to put your love?*" Now, God often places questions in our path to lead us deeper into His Word. But I disregarded the question and carried on the conversation.

Sometime later, I was talking about the food I love. Again I heard, "*Is that where I told you to put your love?*"

The question shocked me. I was puzzled. Stumped by my inability to understand, I opened up my Bible. Turning to Matthew 22:37–39, I was reminded of where we're to put our love.

We're supposed to love God, our neighbor, and our self. That means there's literally no other place on earth, no other thing, no other element that should be given our love. The definition of love is *defined by God*. Where we can place it is *defined by God*. When we define love and put our own stamp on it, we remove the value from love itself.

Pondering that profound but simple message, I began to learn a new definition for love. Pondering brought even deeper questions. *How does love operate?* God's answer was in 1 John 2:15. In it, God says to love not the world, neither the things that are in the world. And if any man loves the world, the love of the Father is not in him.

> *Do not love this world nor the things it offers you, for when you love the world, you do not have the love of the Father in you.*
> (1 John 2:15, NLT)

Reading and digesting that passage was a blast of God's truth. God flipped my reality by confessing His definition. I should not be loving the things of the world. I shouldn't be saying, "I love those shoes; I love that food; I love that song." Instead, I should be saying "I love God, I love those people, and I love myself." The only time love should be brought up in a conversation is when I'm talking about people, God, or myself.

Here's the deal…

Wrong mindedness comes from wrong definitions.
Know the definition.
Then you'll know what to do.

Perfect Parallel

I walked away from that day, and that understanding of love completely changed. There are definitions we don't want in our lives. As long as we use our definitions, we'll produce wrong results, based on wrong beliefs. We need to know what God's definitions are, each step of our walk, each and every day.

God is the One who defines the words, not our culture, not where you were raised, and not what you were instructed. Wrong definitions produce wrong results.

So, while I was transforming and morphing from a regular man, a natural man, to a supernatural man of God, I needed to follow God's supernatural definitions. My language needed to be in line with my beliefs, so my behavior would be in line with God's Word. Walking away with that revelation helped me plot a new course. I began to declare that I'm born of love, a son of love. I declared that my love was aimed at those three only:

> *God.*
> *My neighbor.*
> *Myself.*

Let me illustrate…

Each year I was in prison, I suffered extreme emotional pressure to be depressed during the holidays, as I was away from my children. Though I declared the prayer of Jabez, that God would not use me to cause harm, He would bless me indeed, expand my territory, and His Hand would always be with me and keep me from evil, my tormented mind realized it was my decisions that forced me to be away from my family. I was the person who'd become a lawless thug, who'd been locked away in a cage for a decade. I was the father who'd remained absent from his children, missing out on Christmas mornings, summer vacations, birthdays, and basketball games.

Wrestling with the implications of this stuff, my heart would go to a dark place, realizing that I had caused so much pain for my kids. The holidays became oppressive. Each year I'd push through them, then deal with it again and again and again.

During one of those seasons, I asked God, "How do I love myself?" I still saw myself as a criminal, a brutal thug, a gang leader. I told Him, "God, you showed us in Your Word how to love our neighbor. And then you told us to love our neighbor as ourselves. But how do I love myself? What is Your definition of loving myself?"

I waited. I listened. Inside my spirit, I heard these two words, repeated over and over:

Perfect parallel.
Perfect parallel.

What is that? I wondered. I knew I'd read that somewhere, *perfect parallel.* As I studied it out, I saw the perfection of God's design revealed. In His Bible, there is always going to be a *perfect parallel* that will show me exactly how to do something.

Romans 1:20 is a great example. It speaks of how spiritual things and the invisible things are clearly seen and understood by the things that are made. Empowered by that, I climbed into Luke 10, starting with verse 25, where it clearly defined the perfect parallel.

> *And, behold, a certain lawyer stood up, and tempted him, saying, Master, what shall I do to inherit eternal life? He said unto him, What is written in the law? how readest thou? And he answered and said, Thou shalt love the Lord thy God with all thy heart, and with all thy soul, and with all thy strength, and with all thy mind; and thy neighbor as thyself. And he said unto him, Thou hast answered right: this do, and thou shalt live. But he, willing to justify himself, said unto Jesus, And who is my neighbor?*
>
> (Luke 10:25–29, KJV)

As Luke continues, God reveals His answer to the way we should love a neighbor.

> *And Jesus answering said, A certain man went down from Jerusalem to Jericho, and fell among thieves, which stripped him of his raiment, and wounded him, and departed, leaving him half dead. And by chance there came down a certain priest that way; and when he saw him, he passed by on the other side. And likewise a Levite, when he was at the place, came and looked on him, and passed by on the other side. But a certain Samaritan, as he journeyed, came where he was; and when he saw him,*

> *he had compassion on him, and went to him, and bound up his wounds, pouring in oil and wine, and set him on his own beast, and brought him to an inn, and took care of him. And on the morrow when he departed, he took out two pence, and gave them to the host, and said unto him, Take care of him: and whatsoever thou spendest more, when I come again, I will repay thee. Which now of these three, thinkest thou, was neighbor unto him that fell among the thieves? And he said, He that showed mercy on him. Then said Jesus unto him, Go, and do thou likewise.*
>
> (Luke 10:30–37, KJV)

When I read "go and do likewise," it reminded me of the words, *perfect parallel.* In a flash, I understood. *So, the perfect parallel of the way to love yourself is the way that this Good Samaritan loved his neighbor!*

But how would I do that? First, I'd need to separate my *spirit man* from my *flesh man*, so that my spirit man could represent the Good Samaritan, while my flesh man represented the one who fell among thieves on the way to Jericho. At that moment, I felt the clarion call on my life—the Word of God is sharper than any two-edged sword, possessing the ability to divide asunder and to discern the thoughts and intents of the heart.

The Word started to divide my spirit man from my flesh man. I was shown that the Samaritan—representing the spirit man—went to the place where the flesh fell among thieves, as a result of being lured away from Jerusalem, which represents the place of peace. (The word "Jerusalem" actually means the place of peace or the foundation of peace (Strong's Concordance).

So, the flesh man left the foundation of peace to venture to a place called Jericho. Being attracted to that place, he went on a pathway that gave room for his enemies to steal from him and leave him half-dead. This was the perfect parallel. The Samaritan intentionally journeyed there, armed with oil and wine. Why? He was looking to find someone who had been harmed, so he could help them heal. The Samaritan went in pursuit of repairing the breach. He went in pursuit of fixing the things that were broken. In this, God was showing me that my appetites had taken me into the wrong environments, where I was harmed and hurt, where my most precious treasures were lost.

The way to love myself, I found, was to take on the behavior of the Good Samaritan. Pursue areas in life where I'd failed, where things were lost. Pursue those things with the healing Word of God, the mercy and love of God that would take away the toxins and pour in the healing agents necessary so that I could be healed.

Taking on the same mentality as the Good Samaritan also meant a supreme willingness to sacrifice whatever is necessary, to put myself on the vehicle that could get me from the place of pain to the place of peace.

Thought by thought, God pounded this message into me.

- Be merciful.
- Pursue change.
- Pursue detoxifying areas where wounds are.
- Search your own heart, where things are exposed.

Utilizing the vehicle of faith in God's Word, the vehicle of God's loving-kindness, and the vehicle of God's plan for my life, I could remove myself from the road of destruction as He places me back on the path of health. The result? I learned to love myself back to life with the promises of God, the Word of God, and from what God's definition of us loving ourselves really looks like.

Right definitions will always create the right outcomes.
But wrong definitions will always create wrong outcomes.

Wrong Definitions, Wrong Outcomes

One final definition that changed everything for me appeared in Luke, chapter 18, and concerned the concept of "good".

In the past, I'd always say, "It was a good day, I had a good time," or "Things are going pretty good," without God's definition of *what is good*. Again, I pursued God. again, God drove me to His Word, to Luke 18:18–19 (KJV).

> *And a certain ruler asked him, saying, Good Master, what shall I do to inherit eternal life? And Jesus said unto him, Why callest thou me good? None is good, save one, that is, God.*

That gave me God's definition of *good*. God is good. And good is God. Anything that is good is only good because it's coming directly from God. Immediately, I was taken back to the very beginning of the Bible when God created the heavens and the earth. After He created everything, He looked at it and saw,

> *It was very good.*
>
> (Genesis 1:31, KJV)

What was He saying? God was saying, *This is what I wanted it to be. This is a representation of Me.*

When we take on the definitions of the Bible, we take on the right definitions. So long as we live by the world's definitions—what mama told us, what our friends think, what we believed because of the neighborhood we grew up in—so long as we take on those definitions we'll be trapped in a never-ending downward spiral.

Wrong definitions lead to wrong results.

We don't want wrong results—and neither does God. But God knows for us to receive the right results we've got to start with right definitions. That's why He gave us His Word. That's why He gave us His Spirit. And that's why He gave us Himself.

So long as you continue to pursue doing things the way you've always done them, you'll experience the same outcomes you've always had. Nothing will change. However, if you choose instead to read the Bible as if it was a book of definitions, you'll find that not only do you change and morph from the natural to the supernatural, but the way you affect and impact the world around you will change also. God will get glory from you having the right definitions in your story.

It wasn't comfortable, attempting to change the definitions I'd believed for so long. Because I knew there existed a definition that was absolute, it created tension in my mind. But it was necessary. New definitions change everything.

If we line up our words with God's Word, no longer will our lives be average or mediocre. No longer will we be held hostage by old behaviors. Instead, we'll experience a radical shake-up, and become the raw material for becoming His masterpiece, the man or woman He created us to be.

The Bible says God is the Potter, and we are His clay (Isaiah 64:8). To become His clay, we must allow the definitions we believe to change. We must choose to be comfortable with being uncomfortable. Even though it might feel like we're fighting old ways and learning to walk all over again, it's worth it to endure the discomfort of change rather than deal with the pain of staying the same.

CHAPTER SIX

• • • • • •

BEING COMFORTABLE WITH
BEING UNCOMFORTABLE

During my long stay, behind the razor wires, weightlifting became a part of my daily routine. I began lifting weights the day I was incarcerated and continued regularly lifting for a while after I was released.

One of the things I learned as a result of consistent weightlifting was how to grow comfortable with being uncomfortable. Although I worked out a different body part group each day, I lived in perpetual pain. If I exercised my legs on Monday, my arms on Tuesday, and my chest on Wednesday, by the time I got around to Thursday, my legs were aching. By Friday, my arms were throbbing. And on Saturday, my chest was screaming at me. And yet because I consistently endured the process of being in pain in weight-lifting, the process taught me that the only way I would receive continuous gains was to get to a place where pain could be endured.

The place where I was completely comfortable with being uncomfortable.

There were seasons where my arms were so exhausted, so fatigued, so dog-tired that I could hardly pick up anything. There were times when my legs were so exhausted that if I dropped something, I'd walk away from it because bending down produced too much pain.

The soreness and the pain and discomfort were extreme. But after living with the pain, after staying uncomfortable for a while, I came to the place where it was normal for there to be pain in some area of my body. To me, growing comfortable with being uncomfortable wasn't a weakness. It was a sign of strength. It took guts and fortitude. It was a decision to endure the process of change.

Relation-*Ships*

One day, as I was meditating on the Word of God, I flipped to Matthew 4:4 (KJV), where I read this passage about Jesus:

> *But he answered and said, "It is written, Man shall not live by bread alone, but by every word that proceedeth out of the mouth of God.*

I read and re-read those words over and over again, mulling and meditating on the verse. *If it proceeds,* I thought, *then there must be a process.* As I pondered this, I thought about the process I was undergoing, allowing the Word of God to morph me from a wicked man into a godly man. *Since there is a process,* I decided, *that means there are going to be both seasons of comfort and seasons of discomfort.*

The reality hit me all at once. Not only would there be seasons of comfort and discomfort, I realized—some seasons would be more uncomfortable than others. That meant

I would have to prepare for discomfort, prepare to persevere, to continuously be uncomfortable so that I could continuously see gains as I pursued my season of change.

That was a big deal. Because I'd been lifting weights because I understood how weightlifting and body shaping made it necessary for there to be pain and discomfort to experience gain, discomfort felt good. The discomfort felt necessary.

Day by day, my demeanor, my attitude changed. A new vision was born. *This feels like what I'm supposed to be doing. So what if I experience pain! I'm ready to live in discomfort to see who and what God originally planned for me to be. I'm a warrior in training! I'm ready to push through all the pain and finish the process.*

My commitment to change made the pain worth it. Over time, I began to understand that the struggle was proof that I was changing. Plus, God gave me His Holy Spirit, who is called "The Comforter" in John 14:26 because He knew we'd have uncomfortable seasons to push through.

Process creates change. The Bible states in Genesis, chapter 6 that Noah found grace in the eyes of God after God had decided earlier that everything about man was wicked, and judgment was about to be rained down upon the whole earth. But God chose to show favor towards Noah, through His painstaking process.

> *And God said unto Noah, The end of all flesh is come before me; for the earth is filled with violence through them; and, behold, I will destroy them with the earth. Make thee an ark of gopher wood; rooms shalt thou make in the ark, and shalt pitch it within and without with pitch. And this is the fash-*

ion which thou shalt make it of: The length of the ark shall be three hundred cubits, the breadth of it fifty cubits, and the height of it thirty cubits. A window shalt thou make to the ark, and in a cubit shalt thou finish it above; and the door of the ark shalt thou set in the side thereof; with lower, second, and third stories shalt thou make it. And, behold, I, even I, do bring a flood of waters upon the earth, to destroy all flesh, wherein is the breath of life, from under heaven; and every thing that is in the earth shall die. But with thee will I establish my covenant; and thou shalt come into the ark, thou, and thy sons, and thy wife, and thy sons' wives with thee. And of every living thing of all flesh, two of every sort shalt thou bring into the ark, to keep them alive with thee; they shall be male and female. Of fowls after their kind, and of cattle after their kind, of every creeping thing of the earth after his kind, two of every sort shall come unto thee, to keep them alive. And take thou unto thee of all food that is eaten, and thou shalt gather it to thee; and it shall be for food for thee, and for them. Thus did Noah; according to all that God commanded him, so did he.
(Genesis 6:13–22, KJV)

Reading God's process in those verses overwhelmed me. He actually handed down to this one man, to Noah, instructions to save mankind. The details define not only Noah constructing a massive boat, an ark, but also calling in all the animals of the earth, and figuring out which animals were clean and which were unclean.

God's to-do list was enormous! Surely the amount of work would swamp the minds and break the backs of most men. But there remained one incredible detail I was shocked to discover—the man's name, Noah's name, meant *rest.*

Stop for a moment and savor that thought. Noah's name means rest—yet God hands down to him an enormous amount of work. God's final instructions to Noah involve the details necessary for him to build a wooden ship that will overcome the severe judgment the rest of the world will soon receive.

As my mind pondered this wooden boat, Noah's Ark, I compared this ship to my relation-*ship* with God. On the inside, I saw my relationship equivalent to Noah building an ark that would rise above the judgment of the world. I was creating my relation-*ship* with God, from the words He said about me—words that caused me to not only rise above the judgment of the wicked of this world but into His grace.

Words that allowed me to enter into the place where I saw myself the way He saw me.

Up Where I Belong

Believing this, my frustration with God's process turned to anticipation, then to inspiration. It became easier for me to not only follow the instructions but to see what I was building was a relation-*ship* with the Father, a life-saving connection that had been ripped apart as a result of sin but was restored because of Jesus.

Like Noah, I was building back the things that were broken as a result of bad decisions. Though I was lifting weights, applying pressure and resistance towards change, and though the pain, at times, was excruciating, the pain I felt at the thought of *not* changing was even more unbearable. I couldn't just flip a switch and see the change. Deep inside, a twisted part of me still wanted to be the "old" Art. Ultimately, I discerned that the change was worth it—to fall short would make it worthless. To endure the pain of change, rather than the pain of staying the same, was the goal.

Over and over, my thoughts brought me back to Noah. To the discomfort, he must have experienced. I began to ask God, "*How uncomfortable could it have made Noah, knowing he's building a boat on dry land—a boat bigger than a football field—when it has never, ever rained?*" Noah must have felt like the laughingstock of the whole community. Surely people thought he was nuts. He'd become the butt of every joke. The humiliation and discomfort must have been enormous!

Thinking about that, it became clear to me that Noah had to become comfortable with being uncomfortable, for a long time. Not only that—he had to become comfortable with rejection. Peter 2:5 (KJV), tells us that Noah was a preacher of righteousness.

> *And spared not the old world, but saved Noah the eighth person, a preacher of righteousness, bringing in the flood upon the world of the ungodly.*

Now, you might think a preacher of righteousness would be able to help people transition from wicked to upstanding. But Noah couldn't save anybody—not his friends, not his neighbors, only his family members and a ship full of animals, which means he faced constant mocking, ridicule, and rejection from people. *Who is this crazy man, talking about rain falling from the sky?*

Noah's sanity must have been hanging by a thread, which means Noah grew comfortable with being uncomfortable. Wouldn't you be uncomfortable knowing God planned to rain down judgment and destruction on your friends and neighbors? And He means for you to inherit the entire earth?

Noah was forced to endure a long season of discomfort. Still, Noah followed God's instructions and found rest in the midst of discomfort.

As I meditated on the things necessary for God to change me, I knew there would be some uncomfortable seasons when I had to do the right thing when everyone around me was doing the wrong thing. I knew there would be pain and anxiety when a part of me was saying, *Do the right thing*, and another part was saying, *Do the wrong thing*. I'd need to muster the strength and courage to climb that hill because something deep inside is telling me this is where I belong. Up here. In the hidden high places. Up with the eagles.

The result of following God's instructions produces a gain. And yet faced with gain or pain, we often panic. When I was lifting weights, as my muscles grew stronger and I experienced gains, those gains would make it easier for me to push further, to stretch to new limits, and endure more pain. Enduring pain requires tenacity. When I went into the penitentiary, I could barely do fifteen pushups. Shortly after being released, I could bench press 415 pounds. That enormous amount of bench press came out of discomfort. The gain came from pain. Progress came out of discomfort.

We all make excuses not to tap into discomfort, don't we? It's a never-ending battle call to choose the comfortable place, the shortcut, the easy thing. On the other hand, if we push through, if we punch past the pain to receive the gain, transformation will come.

Being uncomfortable in life can be scary. Stand firm challenge yourself to step into the fire. Transition out of fear into miraculous change.

Change makes it all worth it.

Risky Behavior

The same is true for another area of discomfort; the discomfort of taking risks.

Faith in God means taking risks. Faith in God means putting it all on the line and not caring if you lose everything. Risk equals reward. Risk equals rising out of bondage. Risk equals transformation.

You don't need to look far to find story after story in the Bible illustrating this. I'm certain it was risky for Abraham to walk his son, Isaac, up a mountain to kill him, uncertain if his wife would agree with him following God's will. It was risky for Noah to build a ship on dry land and preach righteousness to people who were rejecting him and thinking he was crazy.

In Matthew 21:2–3 (KJV), Jesus reveals this same concept:

> *Saying unto them, Go into the village over against you, and straightway ye shall find an ass tied, and a colt with her: loose them, and bring them unto me. And if any man say ought unto you, ye shall say, The Lord hath need of them; and straightway he will send them.*

Jesus tells the disciples they will find a donkey tied to a certain place, that they need to bring the donkey back, and if anyone asks them to say that the Lord has need of it. Not only is that risky behavior—that is uncomfortable behavior. Sure, you know God has given you these instructions; you know God has given you the strength to endure whatever happens as a result, and you know God is the One bringing about the results of the instruction. But while you're performing this bold act of faith, your heart is pounding because you know there's a risk...

- There's a risk the donkey won't be there.
- There's a risk the owner will be reluctant to let you take the donkey.
- There's a risk you'll be arrested for stealing the donkey.

However, every time we choose to take risks, and show God we have faith in Him, no matter what the circumstance, there's going to be great gain. When we do our little portion, God does His big portion. His big portion produces great gains. So, although the risk is uncomfortable, although the process is uncomfortable, although sometimes the way people perceive our behavior and respond is uncomfortable if we'll grow *comfortable with being uncomfortable* God can use us to fulfill His vision. And our choice to trust Him can affect the entire world around us.

As we morph, as we undergo the process of taking off the old and putting on the new, discomfort arises. We experience spiritual battles. We wage war against our old strong held mindsets. We overcome the enemies around us—the demonic, the satanic, but also the enemies *within* us.

So, the question is, *Will you choose the pain of change over the pain of staying the same?* Because both require pain. The pain of staying the same grows worse and worse. The pain of change grows easier and easier.

God wants us to take bold risks out of our comfort zone. When we take bold risks for the glory of God, He empowers us, leads us, and equips us with His spiritual weaponry. And with His weaponry, we cease being victims.

And become overcomers.

Unseen Opponents

As I morphed, the discomfort I experienced was not discomfort from fear, people's opinions, or external sources. The majority of the discomfort became *me disliking the sounds of me.* It was me disliking my new thoughts, my new choices, my new ways. It was me not wanting to sacrifice my old behaviors.

The war I was really fighting with was with *me.*

Too often, we come to a place where we're unwilling to fight with ourselves to allow God to manifest our change. If we could stand back and look at the real fight, we'd see that the battlefield is the mind, and our true enemies can be found lurking there…

In inner me.

As I grew in my fight of faith and my battle to change, I discovered that the majority of my battle was with an unseen but familiar opponent…

With *me.*

CHAPTER SEVEN

• • ● • •

THE ENEMY OF INNER ME

It's a glorious day when a new child is born.

When a child is born, the newborn is oblivious to the world around them. The world is new and overwhelming. The child is taking in light, sound, scent, and information it has never seen or experienced before. It's learning to discern security by the way a person holds them. It's learning about life.

What drives the child to learn are its *appetites*. An appetite for comfort is the first reason a child cries when it feels pain. Noticing that its cry stopped the pain, the cry becomes one of its first tools, something to curb the appetites. As we grow from newborn infants into small children, teenagers, and adults, our appetites drive us. Our internal appetites control our behavior.

As an evil individual, my appetites were enormous and always raging. My appetites were my old ways of thinking. Old systems of belief. Old systems of behavior. As I grew in God's ways, I began to identify and expose these old appetites as my enemies. If I could defeat these enemies, I could cut them off. If I cut them off, I could be morphed into the man God created me to be.

As I grew, my appetites were transformed. As I changed and learned, God revealed that my real enemy was *inner me.*

Hunger Drives

The place God revealed the identity of my real enemy was in Scripture, in a passage found in Matthew 5:6 (KJV).

> *Blessed are they which do hunger and thirst after righteousness: for they shall be filled.*

Let's talk about hunger.

Hunger is an appetite borne from a system of absence and fulfillment. Without absence, there is no hunger. Absence in our bellies creates discomfort, and discomfort creates a demand to fill and then releases that feeling of hunger. Does that sound deep and hard to understand? Let me make it easy.

The physical body has systems. Each of us has a reproductive system and digestive system. My digestive system is where I take in food. If I have no food and no nutrients so that blood can transfer the nutrients throughout the body, my digestive system recognizes the absence and begins to release something out of its discomfort called hunger. Hunger then drives me to feed the system.

Hunger drives. Appetites drive.

Once the system makes a demand because of something being absent, it causes us to go into pursuit mode. Without pursuit, there is no desire. But if there is desire, there will always be a pursuit.

Appetites drive pursuit. Pursuit is a behavior. Every behavior is a result of a belief. And every belief puts us in pursuit of that thing. For instance, if you believe it's good to be hungry for food, but it's better to be hungry for a soul mate, you'll find yourself making decisions when it comes to your mate that you wouldn't make when it comes to choosing the best drive-thru hamburger.

Why is that? It's because different appetites, attached to different systems, are arranged differently in us. Because of that, we respond differently.

Bigger appetite, bigger commitment, bigger pursuit.

If I'm committed to feeding only myself, I may take a shovel and dig a hole to get paid enough to feed myself. But, if I need to feed my family, I'll take a shovel and move a mountain. My commitment is bigger because my appetite is bigger.

When man first was on the earth, way back in the caveman days, man needed to become gangster enough to fight with a lion, to battle a bear. What was necessary to get them in fighting mode?

Hunger. Hunger fueled them. Hunger made them ready to fight. Hunger made them ready to risk their lives.

Right Appetite, Right Action

Appetites control us. But our appetites must be arranged. This means I have appetite one, appetite two, appetite three, appetite four. What is your number one appetite? I know for a fact that most of the world's number one appetite is for money. Because it's their number one appetite, money will drive them to work forty or more hours a week, knocking out eight-hour shifts each day. But when they go to church, if the service goes over two hours, folks get upset because they're getting robbed of their Sunday hamburger or their team's NFL football game. That tells you that on the inside, their appetite for money is bigger than their appetite for God.

Our appetite exposes our condition. It exposes how we arrange things in our list of priorities. And when you arrange things wrong, you reverse Scripture. Reverse Scripture? How do you do that?

For every truth, there is an opposite truth. If scripture says...blessed, prosperous, happy, to be envied "are those who hunger and thirst for righteousness; for they shall be filled" (Matthew 5:6, NKJV). It also says, Cursed are they who hunger and thirst after unrighteousness; for they shall never be satisfied (Reversed).

One is the blessing. The other, in reverse, is the curse. The breakdown is that our appetites determine the outcome. What we didn't know when we were born was, we'd be led and driven by our appetites. A child cries because of their appetite for food, their appetite for relief from pain.

Appetites are important. The right appetite, the right outcome. The wrong appetite, the wrong outcome.

Right Appetite, Wrong Position

Let's examine the reverse of that—right appetite in the wrong position equals wrong outcome.

If eating a juicy sandwich is more important than spending some time with God, it's the right appetite in the wrong position, and it reverses the scripture. By reversing Scripture, we're never satisfied. Our potential prosperity gives way to poverty. Our peace gives way to problems, and our overall health gives way to pain.

Did you know there is such a thing as a false absence? A false absence means that something you believe is gone, isn't gone.

The Bible says God has given us *all* things that pertain to life and Godliness. What does that mean? They're already ours. But what the enemy attempts to do, to drive us into wrong outcomes, is to make us believe there's absence.

In Genesis, chapter 3, it reveals how the Devil goes to Adam and Eve saying,

> "...*Has God indeed said, 'You shall not eat of every tree of the garden'?"*
> "...*You will not surely die. For God knows that in the day you eat of it your eyes will be opened, and you will be like God, knowing good and evil."*
>
> (Genesis 3:1, 4–5, NKJV)

What is the Devil trying to tell Adam and Eve? *There is something missing.* There's something absent. There's something you don't have that you really want. But he's lying. It's a false absence because it's already there. They already know good and evil. They know God who is good, and they are talking to evil. However, the enemy tempted Adam and Eve to stop believing they possessed something, which they already possessed.

He does the same thing with you and me.

Do you know what happens when you demonstrate confidence in the Devil and his words, rather than confidence in God and His Words? The Matthew 5:6 scripture turns around. You go from the blessed to the cursed because you're demonstrating confidence in a lie creating a territory for an enemy.

TV marketers still do this today. It's on every commercial you see. You see a new car commercial with a pretty girl, and the TV marketers make it seem that if you get this new car, you'll get the girl. We all know it's a lie. But it works. Why? Because the marketers create a belief that something is absent in your life, which gives birth to an appetite to fill that absence.

Every time something reminds you of absence, it's to create or intensify an appetite. What you need to understand is the Devil often tries to gain your belief that something you already have, you really *don't*.

In Matthew, chapter 4, the Bible says Jesus was hungry because He'd been fasting for forty days. He'd been led by the Spirit into the wilderness. So, Jesus had an appetite—Hunger. His almighty digestive system was calling for food. But Jesus, on purpose, was denying His flesh. He was intentionally turning off His appetite.

So, the Devil tried to use that appetite against Jesus. The Devil said, *"...If you are the Son of God, command that these stones become bread" (Matthew 4:3, NKJV).* What is he telling Jesus? He's saying, first of all, I don't believe You're the Son of God. Second, You're hungry, and there's an absence of food in You. The Devil is trying to drive behavior with wrong belief. He's trying to create a belief of absence.

But Jesus flat blasted him with this comeback: "...Man shall not live by bread alone, but by every word that proceeds out of the mouth of God" (Matthew 4:4, NKJV).

Jesus was saying, *I don't live by the flesh appetites alone; I have an appetite for God. I have an appetite to fulfill the Word of God.* As a result, He rejected the Devil's temptation, and then His refusal released a blessing, for the Bible states that the angels came and ministered to Him.

Reject false absence. Reject wrong positioned appetites. Embrace the right outcomes, and you'll be equipped to go forward and thrive.

The Brook That's Dried Up

Another scripture about appetites driving the inner me can be found in 1 Kings, when God came to a starving Elijah and said, Go to Cherith. There's a brook there, and you will drink from the brook, and the ravens of the air will bring you food (1 Kings 17:2–4).

What is God telling Elijah? God's saying, *I know you have an appetite, so if you'll go to this place I'll fill, feed, and supply your appetite.* Elijah followed God's Word. He went to the brook, the birds brought him food, and the brook gave him water.

Next, the Bible says that the brook dried up. When the brook dried up, the voice of the Lord returned. What does that tell you? It tells you that when things become absent, it's so you'll return to God for replenishment for your next assignment. Thus, as soon as the brook dried up, the word of Lord came and told Elijah… Now I want you to go to a widow woman, whom I have commanded to sustain you (1 Kings 17:8–9).

What is God saying? He's saying, *Understand that I can propel you when there's the pursuit of provision. I can move you forward by letting you see that I will supply your appetites. I want to be your **source**. And I can give you assignments if you'll listen to Me rather than the enemy when those appetites arise.*

God has a way that things will come to you. He said in Matthew 6:33 (KJV),

> *But seek ye first the kingdom of God, and his righteousness; and all these things shall be added unto you.*

What a powerful promise! If you turn your pursuit to God, to the things of God, and turn your love to the things

God loves, those other things are going to chase you and be added to you. But, when we reverse Matthew 5:6, those appetites for the world and for the things of the world start to pull you away from God.

False absence is dangerous because it leads us to believe we really don't have what God already gave us. And the way God works is by faith. Faith unlocks grace. When we dig into faith, we get to the place where we have not just an appetite and a desire for God, but we believe we have received even in the absence of any manifestation.

The Devil doesn't want that. He wants you to get to a place of doubt, fear, temptation. The moment someone demonstrates doubt, they demonstrate confidence in what the Devil said rather than what God said. With the false sense of absence, the Devil tries to get us to turn our appetites to his source.

Did you know if you're around your parents long enough, you'll take on their same appetites? You'll have an appetite for wisdom if your mom is going to school at night. You'll have an appetite for laziness if your pop parties all weekend long. You take on the appetite of what is patterned as the norm. Even if it's not what's right, even if it's not what your belief tells you to do, it's what you were trained to do.

The Devil knows how to create appetites where there are none. Every time he tempts you and tells you that you need something, your response should be, *I have that,* or *God already did that for me.*

When the Devil says you're fooling yourself, you're not saved, you need to reply, *Yes, I am saved. I believe the Word of God, Devil!*

What appetite is the Devil tempting you with? What thoughts are attempting to steal your future? And how can you engage the drive that will allow God to direct you in your faith walk?

Wrong Arrangement, Wrong Appetite

Appetites drive us. We need to create them with a purpose. We need to choose intentionally to direct our appetites.

If I mistakenly believe what I'm doing is the result of a right appetite, then in doing it I'll expect to receive a reward. Maybe my reward is a high from drugs or some money out of a shady deal. If I see a reward, the experience fosters that appetite because it solidifies the experience. I become driven to obtain more of the reward.

Why did the fruit Eve ate taste so good? Because sin always feels good for a moment—yet you pay the price for a long time. You hunger and thirst for that reward you experienced, pursuing a "high" without seeing the ultimate cost—until it's too late.

When that happens, there's a wrong arrangement of wrong appetites. A wrong arrangement of wrong appetites creates wrong rewards. Wrong rewards like addictive behavior. Ask yourself:

- What's most important in my life?
- Who or what do I put in the highest place, in first position?

The Bible in Matthew 6:33 says we're to seek first the Kingdom of God and His righteousness. First is God's way. If we put God's Way first, everything else comes in good. If we say, *First is my kids;* then we raise self-centered children who find themselves divorced a lot because we made them the center of the family.

It's crucial that God be first. If God is first, He'll tell us the arrangement of the rest.

Now I know what you're thinking. *Hold on. God so loved man next to Himself so that means I need to love man above other stuff?* Yes! It means we don't love money more than man. It means we don't rob or swindle people of their money because we love the money more than we love them. It means we don't do anything to get the desired result that is contrary to what God would have us do.

The wrong arrangement of wrong appetites is the real enemy of the inner me. When we decide that the things of the world are more important than the things God loves, we've created a wrong arrangement of appetites.

Don't let perverse appetites drive. If you have an appetite for selfish ambition, it will lead you to reclassify people as lesser than you. It will lead you to destructive thinking and destructive behavior. That's why it's important to ask God to elevate us when our appetites drag us down.

God says, *if you love Me, you love them* (John 14:15, 1 John 3:23, KJV). The world says, *If you love money, forget about Him.*

Recently I conversed with a pastor from Liberia. He explained how the Liberian people are dealing with issues. When they become sick, they can't afford to go to the hospital. Their hospitals charge a fee before they begin service. These beautiful people are barely living. "Yet when you come to America," he said, "You see that dogs and cats are treated better than our countrymen." It made him feel like they're lesser than human beings in the sight of some because there's a whole country full of people who feel that dogs and cats are more valuable than people. He thinks of his countrymen dying because they can't afford medical treatment, as he rides down the street in America and sees animal hospitals.

As I mulled the pastor's words, I thought to myself, *It is so true how perverse some things have gotten.* People love animals more than they love each other. The wrong arrangement of appetites is driving entirely too much, causing people to be used by the enemy against one another.

What does the thought of all that unrighteousness create? It creates an absence in me, which creates an appetite for righteousness—a hunger and thirst for virtue. My appetite makes me want to push and fight and struggle to get somebody saved, to heal those who are hurting, to lift my fellow man out of the broken place, to transform somebody's life by introducing them to Grace, Himself.

Why? Because not only is that appetite real—it's because I see the absence that God sees. That's how we were created to be. In God's likeness, in God's image with God's heart.

Society has flipped that. The world makes you feel your new iPhone is worth fighting for instead of your neighbor. Time on social networks and the internet is worth fighting for instead of time spent feeding your faith or with your family.

We need repositioning of our priorities. We need a new hunger.

There is a hunger and a thirst that will produce glorious results. Jesus, Himself, explains it for us, in John 4:31–34 (KJV).

> *In the meanwhile his disciples prayed him, saying, Master, eat. But he said unto them, I have meat to eat that ye know not of. Therefore said the disciples one to another, Hath any man brought him ought to eat? Jesus saith unto them, My meat is to do the will of him that sent me, and to finish his work.*

What is Jesus saying? He's saying, I hunger and thirst for righteousness. I hunger and thirst so that things can be made right. I hunger and thirst to do the Will of God in the earth to help humanity, to help the hurting, to bring healing to the broken, to bring change to the lives of people.

I hunger for that. I thirst for that. If I hunger for the wrong appetites that hunger becomes the poison to my purpose. And the enemy of me becomes the inner me.

The Blind Side

We all have appetites, driving us to some degree. Some have right appetites, appetites that elevate. Some have wrong appetites, appetites that diminish. Our right appetites drive us to press on toward the prize, toward the upward call of God. Our wrong appetites drive us to places of pain like the man who fell among thieves in The Good Samaritan story. But instead, the Spirit of God is here to possess our appetites, and turn them towards victory if we'll just do one thing...

Turn them over to Him.

Once I'd overcome my wrong appetites, and turned my appetite to Jesus, I began to experience an intimate oneness with my Father God. That oneness lifted my gaze toward a vision of my next necessary transformation point. To further morph, I needed to dig out the negative roots if I expected to eliminate the bad fruit in my life.

How would that be done? How would I nurture fertile ground when the ground I'd tilled in the past was poisoned with pain?

— By digging down into the original issue.
— By pursuing the root.

CHAPTER EIGHT

• • • • • •

PURSUIT OF THE ROOT

Symp·tom

sim(p)təm/*noun*

> 1. *a physical or mental feature / indicating a condition of disease or illness, particularly such a feature that is apparent to the patient.*
> 2. *a sign of the existence of something, especially of an undesirable situation.*
>
> ("Symptom" 2019)

Few things frustrate people more than feeling a cough or a cold coming on. Experiencing a tightness in the throat or an itchy runny nose is a sign that an illness is surfacing, maybe even the flu. Those signs of illness are *symptoms.*

When someone says they've caught a cold or the flu, they're defining the source of the symptoms. But when it comes time to address the symptom, instead of going after the *root,* the origin, or the source, most go after the *fruit.* They ask the physician or their pharmacist to prescribe a medication that will remove the symptoms. Stopping the symptoms is how we medicate the problem.

Living in a society that is bound to the "medicate mindset" hinders our process to healing. We're tempted by the shortcut, instead of cleansing ourselves of the problem once and for all time. It's difficult to eliminate invisible roots because the focus instead is often only on the visible fruit.

God wants us to pursue the root of our negative issues. God isn't looking for band-aids on bullet wounds, quick fixes, or short-term pharmaceuticals. God wants us to get down in the trenches and allow Him to eliminate the problem completely.

God wants total victory. A "medicate" mentality says *shut down the symptom.*

But an "eliminate" mentality says *kill it at the source.*

Fresh Fruit for Rotting Vegetables

Here's a powerful truth for your brain to download… there will always be a root attached to the fruit in our lives. Before we see fruit, there's a seed and invisible root.

Think of the negative beliefs in your life—fear, insecurity, condemnation, discouragement—like roots. Bad, rotting fruit is the behavior that follows. The enemies main job is to paralyze you from seeing this hanging fruit actually rotting on the vine. But, if you dig at the roots, and pursue an answer from God as to what the root of the issue is, you can not only stop it for a season…

You can stop it *forever.*

A "medicate" mentality is the equivalent of mowing a massive grassy field full of dandelions, just to cut the weeds down. Although it looks healthy for a short span, not only are the weeds going to pop up again, but they're going to sow more seeds and grow into more weeds choking out more of the grass. Year, after year, after year.

The root shapes the fruit. And every issue, every problem, every symptom has a root. The only way to eliminate fruit is to attack it at its root. Roots grow in the dark, in an unseen realm, hidden for long periods of time. Let me illustrate.

I read once about a bamboo that grows as high as ninety feet tall. It grows extremely fast—as much as thirty-six inches in a single twenty-four-hour period. This growth doesn't happen overnight though. This bamboo grows roots for seven years before the bamboo breaks ground, bursting forth into the visible realm where it can be seen. Until then, the bamboo remains invisible.

Like that bamboo, our issues have the potential to grow massive roots for a long period of time, unseen, before eventually manifesting themselves as full-blown toxic influences, toxic emotions, and toxic behaviors, in the form of fruit. But, if you attack the root in its hidden place, even in its secluded form you can stop it from sprouting, from blooming, and bearing fruit.

The Bible tells us in Hebrews 12:15 (KJV),

> *Looking diligently lest any man fail of the grace of God; lest any root of bitterness springing up trouble you, and thereby many be defiled.*

Think about this for a moment. If you're plagued by bitterness, it was born and developed in darkness, in secret, in the invisible realm, before bitterness sprang up to trouble you. Every fruit has a root. And every root began with a seed.

In the Hebrews, chapter 12, the root of bitterness could not grow bitter without first having been offended. Thus, the root of bitterness was developed *after* the seed of offense. Something was said, something was done, a person became offended, and walked away harboring that offense. They concealed it within them as the seed of unforgiveness, and it began to develop the roots of bitterness. Those roots may have stayed concealed within them for days, for years, even decades before they ever bore fruit.

When I think about the bamboo, I think to myself, *Is there anything attempting to grow roots in me? Is there anything in my life bearing fruit that will be destructive?*

Acknowledging the fruit is a start. I then ask God to show me the root of my problems. As an overcomer, and being more than a conqueror, I want to see the origin, the birth, the seed-planting event. If it's a root of bitterness, He will reveal the moment I became offended, how I held onto the offense and quietly walked away offended, how the roots of bitterness began to form because I refused to forgive.

Seeing the root, the behavior my poisonous seed created, my first impulse is always to be defensive. Say some guy offends me, my default defense mechanism will be to stay away from that guy or any guy who reminds me of the offender. My defense mechanism automatically classifies the offender. Soon, I'm cutting myself off from guys like him, then from everybody else. All that defense mechanism is doing is permitting the root to grow further, grow deeper so that bitterness can drive me away from hearing God's voice, the voice of forgiveness.

The scripture in Hebrews, chapter 12, also says look *diligently*. We're called upon to look diligently, so we don't fail to receive the blessing of God's grace in our lives, all because of a root that bore fruit. Let's go back to the beginning of this Chapter: the sneeze and cough. How do we eliminate the symptoms?

- Pursue the root.
- Replace the temptation to focus on medicating.
- Don't reach for a four-hour fix from a cough, a six-hour sniffle stop.
- Eliminate.
- Don't medicate.

I want the symptoms gone forever, not gone for a few hours, a day, a season. And I want to know the *reason* that symptom showed itself and became visible.

Judge a Tree by the Fruit

My story—the story this book is sharing with you, explaining how the Word of God morphed me from a wicked man to a God-fearing man—is my pursuit of the root, which allowed God to bear fruit.

I wasn't created to bear bad fruit. Neither were you. We were both created for a higher purpose. God's power can change us—but change is always going to begin in the invisible, in following the pursuit of the root of the matter.

In Matthew 15:13 (KJV), it says:

> *But he answered and said, Every plant, which my heavenly Father hath not planted, shall be rooted up.*

God, Himself, always pursues the root of the issue. Scripture tells us to judge a tree by the fruit it bears. A good man out of the good treasure of his heart brings forth good things, and a wicked man out of the evil treasure of his heart brings forth wicked things. God's Word digs down and goes after the root of the issue. As His spirit-filled masterpieces, we need to have a "pursuit of the root" mentality—a pursuit of the root of the issue.

Seeds are the source of all fruit. A single seed of a thought gives birth to every action. The thought seed first makes roots that form beliefs, and then those beliefs give birth to our behavior. That single seed is the starting place. It may have grown into a field full of roots and then bushels of fruit, but it all started in a single seed. That single seed can grow into a tree bursting with ripe apples, each of which carries more seeds producing more trees. In fact, it's impossible to look at a single seed and see how far-reaching are the offspring it can produce.

There are more than seven billion people on Earth. Each of those people began with the single seed of a man incubated in a woman, born into a single child. It's impossible to determine how many more will be born from that first seed. That's why we must eliminate a seed either before it takes root or attack it afterward to eliminate the roots.

Whatever you're not pursuing won't change. What you don't pluck out of the ground now won't be eliminated. You can cut down dandelions, but they will sprout again. We need to address the dark heart of issues by addressing the roots. Symptoms will return if they're not rooted out.

What's the best way to pursue a root? Go back to the first time it happened. Return to the first time that issue occurred. Unlock the system, which created that behavior. Eliminate the roots that allow it to reproduce.

Inside each seed is a system of reproduction. When you're attacking the root, you're attacking its ability to reproduce. Don't allow the seed to take root. Don't raise a heart garden filled with bitterness, unforgiveness, strife, and death.

The seed of one thing can produce bad fruit in another season. Whatever root you don't pursue is going to come back later.

- Bigger.
- Stronger.
- More destructive.
- Harder to kill.

I wasn't born thinking I wanted to grow up and become a thug, a criminal, a drug dealer, or an evil, violent man. I was born thinking, *I want to grow up and be something great.* Just like every other child, I had dreams of doing marvelous things. Somewhere along the line, the seed was sown that changed the trajectory of my life. Those seeds were watered consistently and gave birth to fruit containing more bad seeds.

Bad seeds kill great dreams. Bad seeds grow into a bad future, in the fertile soil of a bad heart. God, however, revealed something different. God showed me that the pursuit of the root was the genuine pursuit of change.

If I wanted Him to change the trajectory of my life—to morph me from something wicked, something evil, something ungodly, into something God, Himself ordained—I'd have to turn my pursuit to the root of the issue. If I wanted to kneel before Almighty God and stand up as a different man, I'd have to lay all that bad fruit on the altar.

The grace of God is available. You have probably seen a tree whose roots have broken through the sidewalk, cracked through the cement, and continued to grow. That's how the Word of God will work in us to produce, once we choose to pursue the root of our enemies. The Word of God is planted as the seed of success so that it can grow in us, forcing itself to produce, bringing breakthrough after breakthrough in our lives and bearing the most beautiful fruit.

Piercing the Seed and Pounding the Ground

In Mark, chapter 11, there's the story of Jesus speaking to a fig tree. Finding no fruit, nothing but leaves on the tree, Jesus cursed it.

> *And Jesus answered and said unto it, No man eat fruit of thee hereafter forever!*
> (Mark 11:14, KJV)

And then He walked away. The next day, the disciples came by the same tree and were shocked:

> *Now in the morning, as they passed by, they saw the fig tree dried up from the roots. And Peter, remembering, said to Him, "Rabbi, look! The fig tree which You cursed has withered away!"*
> (Mark 11:20–21, NKJV)

That scripture spoke volumes to me, in my pursuit of the root. It revealed the one thing with the ability to pierce through the hard shell of any negative seed, to penetrate through visible fruit, through the branches, stems, and limbs; to pound straight down into the ground, expose the root, and kill it; eliminating it at its source, completely stopping it from ever experiencing another season of bearing fruit.

That one thing…is the spoken Word of God!

In my pursuit of the root, I can either curse the destructive root that is attempting to bear fruit, or the destructive root could curse me.

Pursue the root with tenacity. Pursue the root relentlessly. And pursue the root early, before the tiny acorn becomes a mighty oak.

Chapter Nine

Uprooting Acorns before They Become Oak Trees

As a child, my mom would send me to Eastern Washington to hang out with my grandfather. He was from Louisiana, southern-born and raised, and had a farm behind his house. Strolling grandpapa's farm, I'd see the grapevines and the collard greens he was growing. Often, I'd catch my grandfather out there, pulling up weeds by the roots. The timing was important, he told me, because it's much easier to snatch up weeds when they are tiny than it is to wait for them to grow into something that could choke out the vine.

As I grew, and let the Word of God morph me from one thing into another, I remembered my grandpapa's wise words. In my imagination, I often returned to the things I saw and learned on his farm. It was not only important to snatch up the bad seed early, but it was also important to look thoroughly and pay attention to what was actually growing in your soil. Because what's lurking in your soil could be destructive to the good seed you've sown.

Uprooting bad seeds and weeds keeps the soil fertile. Discovering bad seed early enables you to stop it from growing into something big. And discovered early, a bad seed is easier to remove. For instance, if I was to plant an acorn in the ground, and let it lie in the soil for a week, it would be easy to dig down however deep I planted it and pull up that acorn before the roots have developed. It's easier to pull up those roots than it is to wait for that little acorn to grow into a mighty oak tree.

Minding the Soil

The Word of God spoke to me in a similar way as the wisdom of my grandfather did. From the Word, I learned that anytime something was being sown in my heart that came from the enemy, I needed to go after it early. Forgiveness is a perfect example.

If someone offends me, it's easier to forgive them immediately, than it is to sit and stew in anger for an hour. In fact, if I let that offense brew, that offense is going to not only develop roots—eventually, it will bear fruit.

Even the enemy understands this principle. Look at Matthew 2:1–18 (KJV).

> *Now when Jesus was born in Bethlehem of Judaea in the days of Herod the king, behold, there came wise men from the east to Jerusalem, Saying, Where is he that is born King of the Jews? For we have seen his star in the east, and are come to worship him. When Herod the king had heard these things, he was troubled, and all Jerusalem with him. And when he had gathered all the chief priests and scribes of the people together, he demanded of them where Christ should be born. And they said unto him, In*

Bethlehem of Judaea: for thus it is written by the prophet, And thou Bethlehem, in the land of Juda, art not the least among the princes of Juda: for out of thee shall come a Governor, that shall rule my people Israel. Then Herod, when he had privily called the wise men, enquired of them diligently what time the star appeared. And he sent them to Bethlehem, and said, Go and search diligently for the young child; and when ye have found him, bring me word again, that I may come and worship him also. When they had heard the king, they departed; and, lo, the star, which they saw in the east, went before them, till it came and stood over where the young child was. When they saw the star, they rejoiced with exceeding great joy. And when they were come into the house, they saw the young child with Mary his mother, and fell down, and worshipped him: and when they had opened their treasures, they presented unto him gifts; gold, and frankincense and myrrh. And being warned of God in a dream that they should not return to Herod, they departed into their own country another way. And when they were departed, behold, the angel of the Lord appeareth to Joseph in a dream, saying, Arise, and take the young child and his mother, and flee into Egypt, and be thou there until I bring thee word: for Herod will seek the young child to destroy him.

Press pause on the verse for a moment, and ask yourself: Why does Herod want to get the child young? *Because he wants to get him early, to destroy Him when it's easier to do so.* Let's continue:

> *When he arose, he took the young child and his mother by night, and departed into Egypt: And was there until the death of Herod: that it might be fulfilled which was spoken of the Lord by the prophet, saying, Out of Egypt have I called my son. Then Herod, when he saw that he was mocked of the wise men, was exceeding wroth, and sent forth, and slew all the children that were in Bethlehem, and in all the coasts thereof, from two years old and under, according to the time which he had diligently inquired of the wise men. Then was fulfilled that which was spoken by Jeremiah the prophet, saying, In Rama was there a voice heard, lamentation, and weeping, and great mourning, Rachel weeping for her children, and would not be comforted, because they are not.*

In this instance, the enemy (Herod) decided he would kill every child from the age of two years and younger because he knew that Christ the King was born and that He would raise up and do great things. Herod was attempting to stop Jesus's potential—he acknowledged it would be easier to defeat his enemy earlier, rather than wait until his enemy dug roots in the community, in the society, and sprouted fruit and power against Herod's kingdom. The enemy understands this principle. Attack the seed early, when it's small. Attack quickly before it develops into something big.

As I was undergoing my change, spending time alone with God, learning how to uproot issues from my life, God instructed me in another principle.

Guard the soil.

Guard the Soil

Proverbs speaks to this: there, the Bible tells us to "guard your heart above all else, for it determines the course of your life" (Proverbs 4:23, NLT). If the soil of my heart is clean, it will bear amazing fruit.

Guard the soil, God instructs us.

If we don't mind our soil, if we neglect negative things starting to sprout up inside of us, sooner or later we'll become a host to evil.

The Bible in Matthew 12:35 (KJV), makes this proclamation:

> *A good man out of the good treasure of the heart bringeth forth good things: and an evil man out of the evil treasure bringeth forth evil things.*

If I have a field of soil, I can sow corn intentionally, or I can sow weeds accidentally. If I allow the soil of my heart to receive negative or cynical words, if I let those things stray into my heart, fruit will be born that comes from weeds.

Return to my grandpapa's garden for a moment. Neighbors up the street had dandelions in their yard. The wind would carry the seeds of those dandelions down into my grandfather's garden. There, they'd be planted accidentally even though my grandfather had planted good seed intentionally.

It's a paradox. Sowing nothing doesn't mean that nothing is sown.

Mind the soil. Keep an eye on the soil. Look to see what the enemy has blown in, attempting to choke out your fruit. When you see it, pull it out early when it's young so that it doesn't destroy your harvest.

Think again of the intense battle inside of Herod. In his fear, Herod saw this miracle child would grow into such a mighty enemy that Herod needed to kill every child, just to make certain he killed this one child. The death of that one child would prevent Herod's downfall, and the death of that child became his obsession.

As a new believer, that scripture stirred me. As I developed into a new man, I reversed that Matthew scripture. Instead of attempting to stop what God sent, I intentionally stopped what the enemy sent. I stopped it young. I stopped it early. I dug down for the root and snatched it up. I pulled that acorn out before it became an oak. My relentless pursuit discontinued the opportunity for evil fruit.

Cleansing the Garden

The Book of Proverbs delivers another insightful message about the power of the tongue.

Whenever I'd envision my grandpapa pulling up weeds, I would see him sticking his hand deep down into the soil, to yank out whatever little thing was hiding there. His hand was the soil's guardian. His hand could usher in life or death.

When I read Proverbs 18:21 for the first time, about death and life being in the power of the tongue, I concluded that the tongue was responsible for ushering in life or ushering in death. At stopping life or stopping death. But as I dug a little deeper, into the original words, I discovered the translation of the word "power" means "hand". Scripture is telling us that death and life are in the "hand" of the tongue. My tongue is equivalent to my hand. Like my hand, it can go into my heart and pull up acorns before they become oak trees.

Just as my grandpapa would reach his hand into the soil and grab the bad roots out of the ground, I can use the hand of my tongue to reach into the soil of my heart and remove the seeds of perversities the enemy would utilize.

I dealt with this numerous times, after returning home. When coming home to a new world, there were new things— new technologies, social platforms, the ability to talk to thousands of people on the internet, to have lots of friends and lots of followers. The whole world was wide-open to me. Someone in Europe or Asia could post a video on Twitter, and I could watch it from my living room as it's taking place on the other side of the earth.

But this wide-open world held hidden dangers.

I remember the first time I was exposed to a pornographic image on the web. The moment the pornographic image hit me; I was slammed with horror. I thought to myself, *Wow! How far-reaching is this? How many lives has this image touched, warped, and perverted? How many lives have been twisted and destroyed by this image? And how many more images like this are out there?* Traumatized by this single image, I immediately saw it as an attempt by the enemy to sow the seed of pornography in my mind, to give birth to perversion on the inside of me. And understanding all I had gone through with allowing the Spirit of God to deliver me and God to transform me while I was inside prison, I did what I'd learned immediately.

I shut my eyes to it. Then I said aloud, "In the name of Jesus, I rebuke that image! I cast down that imagination! And I command it to go far from me. I plead the Blood of Jesus to delete its files from my mind, and I render it harmless and ineffective against me!"

The Blood of Jesus cleanses us, inside and out. In the Old Testament, when people sinned, they were directed to kill an animal; shedding the blood of the animal cleansed them from their sins. But when God saw that was not enough, He sent His Son, Jesus to die for our sins, offering Him as an unblemished sacrifice. Jesus' sacrifice freed and unchained us from the toxic lies of the enemy and cleaned our whole lives, inside and out.

Meditating on that sacrifice humbles me, and reminds me of a verse in Isaiah 53:5 (NKJV),

> *But he was wounded for our transgressions, he was bruised for our iniquities: the chastisement of our peace was upon him, and with his stripes we are healed.*

He was wounded for our sins. He was bruised for our appetites to sin. And He cleansed us on the inside and the outside, with His blood.

But how are we cleansed on the *inside* with His blood?

Bruised and Bleeding

The Bible says the soul is in the blood. Leviticus 17 tells us that the soul of an animal was in the blood of the animal when it was sacrificed, and the soul in the blood of the animal paid for the soul of a man who had sinned against God.

*For the life of the flesh is in the blood; and
I have given it to you on the altar to make
atonement for your souls: for it is the blood
that makes atonement, by reason of the life.*
(Leviticus 17:11, WEB)

This takes me back to the word "transgression". As I studied the word "transgression," I discovered that a transgression represents a sin or an act of sin that causes you to miss the mark. But what is a wound? A wound is an open cut in the flesh, where blood bleeds onto the outside of the flesh. What then is a bruise? A bruise is bleeding on the inside.

In Isaiah 53:5, NKJV version, the Bible says, "He was bruised for our iniquities." The word "iniquity" means to be warped or bent in the direction of sin. Therefore, transgression is the act of sin and iniquity is an inside belief system, a way of thought that moves you in the direction of sin. It's an appetite. Iniquity warps us. It's like your car being out of alignment. As soon as you let go of the steering wheel, instead of the car going straight, it bends and warps in the wrong direction.

Jesus was bruised for our iniquities. The shedding of His Blood cleansed us—our inner thoughts and our outer ways. Each time we need to uproot an acorn that's been sown in our heart, His Blood has the power to erase it from our lives. And by erasing it, we let go of the default setting of the past and press toward the mark, His prize.

Paul's message in Philippians stirs this awakening in me.

*Brethren, I count not myself to have appre-
hended: but this one thing I do, forgetting
those things which are behind, and reach-
ing forth unto those things which are before,*

111

> *I press toward the mark for the prize of the*
> *high calling of God in Christ Jesus.*
> (Philippians 3:13–14, KJV)

How do we do that? How do we press toward the mark? By responding with the spoken Word that acts as a hand, that reaches into the heart, and takes away the seed of perversion, before it takes root.

By this method, we uproot acorns before they become oak trees.

Soul Gardening

Once an acorn becomes an oak tree, the same method is necessary to uproot it. Attacking an oak tree, one must be more aggressive. We can't just uproot a mighty tree from the ground with our fists. We must be more strategic.

First, we need to take a chainsaw to the branches. And a chainsaw to the trunk. Digging up the soil a full distance around the trunk to unearth every root comes next. It might even require a bulldozer, to knock that oak tree from the ground, and chains to rip it out of the soil. Attacking the acorn early is how you win back turf. Removing the seed when it's young keeps it from sprouting into a mighty forest, growing and spreading.

Life is meant to be lived intentionally, not accidentally. We are all sowers of seed. We all reap what we sow. We can watch over our heart garden, and keep out the bad seed, or we can bear bad fruit for seasons and generations to come.

Let's face it. The world will always pour seeds of fear. The winds will always spread seeds of discouragement. There will always be seeds of doubt, seeds of unbelief, seeds of evil taking root, attempting to grow something in you, attempting to warp your destiny.

A clean heart doesn't mean it's always going to remain clean. Just like pure soil can be tainted, so can our hearts. A clean heart and clean soil must be maintained to remain clean. The Spirit of God has given us all the tools and spiritual weapons to uproot evil from our lives. The key is living a life that is intentional, rather than accidental.

When Jesus made the decision to be wounded for our transgressions, He knew His Blood would be necessary as payment for our sins. By shedding His Blood, He knew future believers just like you and me, would be able to wield His name as a weapon against the enemy. His Blood would uproot the seeds of the destroyer. His Blood became our protection from the enemy.

We do have a real enemy. Our enemy knows he can create a crisis in our lives, so he sows seeds of bad behavior as widely and often as possible. The sole purpose of our enemy is to sow seeds that create wrong thoughts, wrong beliefs, wrong results. But our enemy's death and destruction are in our hands—The hands of our tongue that operate when we speak God's Word to the root of every issue.

Even with our sins, our transgressions, our iniquities, God can make us new again. Entering boldly before the throne of grace cleanses us. Allowing sin to take root has consequences.

— Those who sow seeds of evil and wickedness want this world to remain cloaked in darkness.
— Those who work and serve in God's garden, like my grandpapa did, serve the kingdom of heaven.
— Those who become His humble servants and the guardians of our gardens are right believers.

CHAPTER TEN

• • • • • •

RIGHT BELIEVING

Just as the butterfly grows wings inside its safe cocoon, so a believer grows wings of faith in their secret place.

A pivotal point in my spiritual development—when I began to grow wings in the cocoon of my metamorphosis—involved the telling of two stories.

Story one was related by a fellow minister, a powerful man of God with a doctorate in psychology. He spoke of seeing a woman on a brightly lit stage, being hypnotized. During her trance-like state, the hypnotist told her, "You're smoking a cigarette." As soon as the woman heard the hypnotist's words, she held two fingers up in the air, and placed them to her lips, as if taking a long, deep drag from a cigarette. The hypnotist then told her, "Now you're done smoking. Take your cigarette and put it out on your arm."

The minister said the woman took her two fingers, moved them to her wrist, and mimed the act of extinguishing a cigarette on her arm. What was amazing, the minister said, was what happened next. Believe it or not, according to the minister, a *blister* formed on the woman's arm—right there on stage, right in front of the entire shocked audience.

Did the minister and the audience hallucinate this bizarre miracle? Or did the woman truly believe she'd been burned and out of her belief, manifest that blister?

This next story concerns a group of struggling students. Seems no matter how hard they studied, no matter how much they focused on their schooling, these children always received D's on their work. D's on their quizzes. D's on their papers. D's on their final grades.

What did the school officials do? As a test, they decided to tell these D students they were on the school honor roll because they were so smart. They even performed a ceremony for the children, saying they had moved up from D's to A's.

Can you guess what happened?

The following three school quarters, these children began to get straight A's.

This was shocking to the testers, the children's parents, and the school officials because it wasn't the motivation of teachers that caused high achieving and it wasn't lowering the grading standards, or bringing in more tutors.

Instead, it was *right believing.*

Believe and Achieve

Right believing was a pivotal change I made, in my walk with God. Neither my efforts nor my actions were the triggers for lifting me out of the pit. It wasn't reading twenty chapters of the Bible a day, watching TBN, or listening to R. W. Shambock on Christian radio. It was *right believing* on the inside, which produced results on the outside.

Right believers will be high achievers. Why? Because the effort of attempting to achieve something doesn't change their beliefs.

The Word of God goes to the root in us. The Word is a discerner of the thoughts and intentions of the heart. Not only does the Word of God *know* the thoughts and intentions of the heart—the Word of God has the power to *change* those thoughts and intentions.

When the thoughts and intentions of our heart change, right thoughts bring the right beliefs. Right beliefs bring the right behaviors. Right behaviors bring right habits, which bring the right outcomes. It's not about achieving. It's about *right believing.*

The day I understood that success was born. God revealed how my belief created behavior without toil. Right believing creates right behavior without stress, without strain, without struggle—without even sweat!

Right believing will create a sweatless victory.

In 2 Corinthians 4:13 (KJV), it says,

> *We having the same spirit of faith, according as it is written, I believed, and therefore have I spoken; we also believe, and therefore speak.*

Reading this verse brought to mind the words of Romans 10:9:

> *That if thou shalt confess with thy mouth the Lord Jesus, and shalt believe in thine heart that God hath raised him from the dead, thou shalt be saved.*

God's definition of believing is this...until you have spoken, you have not believed. Until the belief produces an action that is visible, audible, and effective on earth, it cannot be borne in the life of the person who may have thought it on the inside but didn't believe it enough to speak it or act on it on the outside.

We believe. Therefore, we speak. We have believed; therefore we've spoken.

Right believing is speaking right words consistently—verbally, as well as inaudibly. In fact, our internal talk is the most important conversation we'll have on earth.

Admittedly, I discovered this late in life. I discovered that my internal talk was the root of every action I'd ever taken. Someone would say something, and my thug mind would start racing. *What made him think that? Who does this guy think he is talking to?* And when that thug talk bubbled up on the inside, thuggish behaviors would show up on the outside. Soon, my inner talk became my outer talk. And my outer talk became my outer walk.

Every thought becomes crystallized in action. Every thought wants to be born as a word, and every word wants to be born as a behavior. Every behavior wants to create a habit, and every habit defines our character.

If I pay attention to my thoughts, they'll produce the right beliefs on the inside.

And right beliefs on the inside create the right behavior. Right behavior becomes an inner voice that says, *I believe I can.* This creates a commitment to push through the struggle, to stay on the battlefield until the enemy is eliminated because I believe I can.

But if I believe *I can't,* my negative beliefs create negative actions. Negative beliefs breed discouragement and make it easy for me to surrender, to lay down my sword, to give up on a fight that I could have won.

The spoken Word of God goes to the heart of the issue, right down to the root, by changing what we believe about ourselves.

Word Power

The Bible proclaims that it is God who calls "those things which be not as though they were" (Romans 4:17, KJV). Thus, God looks at darkness and speaks light. And then the darkness changes into light because God believed it when He spoke it, and when He spoke it, He released the power to make it happen.

That's the way all of mankind works. If I lose my keys and say, "I'll never find them," on the inside, my search-engine heart stops looking for them. But if I say instead, "They're lost, but I'll find them," my heart continues to pursue what I believe I can find. As a result, the right believing will create right behavior.

The right behavior will create the right results.

Although those two scenarios are human-based, when I grab hold of what God says about me, supernatural beliefs create supernatural behavior, which gives God the opportunity to perform supernaturally and bring about supernatural outcomes. All as a result of believing in God's supernatural presence.

In fact, the Bible states that all things are possible to him who believes (Romans 8:28). It doesn't say all things are possible to him who accumulates wealth. Or to him who fights and fights forever. Or to him who studies a lot. No—it says all things are possible for him *who believes.*

But believes what?

Believes God. Believes God's Word. Believes God's way. Believes God can be trusted. And believes what God says, God will perform.

Anything God says you can do, you can do. Anything God tells you to do, He empowers you to do it. Everything God tells you to do is so God can perform wonders in your life so that God can display Himself in the earth as a good and loving God because of the way He displayed His goodness in you.

Right believing is at the root of every right outcome. But right believing comes from the internal submission of the Word of God, the Will of God, and the Way of God. Let me tell you about some wrong believing.

After I received Jesus as my Lord and Savior and believed that the Word of God was accurate, I believed that Jesus forgave my sins. The Blood of Jesus cleansed them. Jesus had the supernatural ability to change my behavior—so when it came to old bad habits or destructive ways of thinking, I gave those over to God.

And because of this, I was seeing great victories. However, I still believed that when it came to money, I had to work as hard as possible. I needed to hustle as fast as I could, spend as much energy as possible, and commit to working myself to death if necessary. Because those old ways of believing caused me to keep this portion of my life that pertained to finances out of God's Hands. You can probably guess what happened.

In every other area of life, I saw success. In every area that I gave to God, I saw success, growth, and development. I saw that area begin to morph and change from something stuck in a low place to something that could rise high and see great things at a distance. But in the areas where I kept that old systemic pattern of thought, like my finances, old behaviors continued to be formed and fostered, and those painful old outcomes continued to come back.

Opening my Bible one day, I read the passage in Luke about God giving seed to the sower, bread to the eater, and multiplying every seed sown.

Give, and it shall be given unto you; good measure, pressed down, and shaken together, and running over, shall men give into your bosom. For with the same measure that ye mete withal it shall be measured to you again.

(Luke 6:38, KJV)

Give, and it will be given to you. What goes around comes around. You reap what you sow. But I still didn't believe that if I gave money to the Kingdom of God and the Gospel, that it would bring money back to me. Until that is, I received a revelation from God in Mark 4:26–29 (KJV).

And he said, So is the kingdom of God, as if a man should cast seed into the ground; And should sleep, and rise night and day, and the seed should spring and grow up, he knoweth not how. For the earth bringeth forth fruit of herself; first the blade, then the ear, after that the full corn in the ear. But when the fruit is brought forth, immediately he putteth in the sickle, because the harvest is come.

The gravity of that passage crashed down on me. *Anything can be a seed,* I realized. Not only giving to people—a smile can be a seed! I can sow the seed of laughter by making people smile and laugh and reap a harvest of laughter. Or I can sow financially to the Kingdom of God, knowing that my seed was going to help the helpless, hopeless, and hurting.

Of course, I was helpless and hurting too, and being helped as a result.

But if instead you choose God's way of doing things, and give to the Kingdom of God, now you can go to sleep. Now you can rest. Now there's no struggle. Now there's no toil. In fact, if you go back to Genesis, chapter 3, you'll find that after Adam and Eve originally sinned, toil was born.

> *And the man said, The woman whom thou gavest to be with me, she gave me of the tree, and I did eat. And the LORD God said unto the woman, What is this that thou hast done? And the woman said, The serpent beguiled me, and I did eat. And the LORD God said unto the serpent, Because thou hast done this, thou art cursed above all cattle, and above every beast of the field; upon thy belly shalt thou go, and dust shalt thou eat all the days of thy life.*
> (Genesis 3:12–14, KJV)

The Devil, through the serpent, was trying to take mankind down to a low place. God was raising them up to a high place. They had one tree they were supposed to stay away from, simply as an act of honor, an act of obeying God's command. But the moment they disobeyed was because they believed the lie the Devil told them. When they believed wrong, wrong believing released toil.

> *And I will put enmity between thee and the woman, and between thy seed and her seed; it shall bruise thy head, and thou shalt bruise his heel. Unto the woman he said, I will greatly multiply thy sorrow and thy conception; in sorrow thou shalt bring forth*

children; and thy desire shall be to thy hus-
band, and he shall rule over thee. And unto
Adam he said, Because thou hast hearkened
unto the voice of thy wife, and hast eaten of
the tree, of which I commanded thee, say-
ing, Thou shalt not eat of it: cursed is the
ground for thy sake; in sorrow shalt thou eat
of it all the days of thy life; Thorns also and
thistles shall it bring forth to thee; and thou
shalt eat the herb of the field; In the sweat
of thy face shalt thou eat bread, till thou
return unto the ground; for out of it wast
thou taken: for dust thou art, and unto dust
shalt thou return.

(Genesis 3:15–19, KJV)

Why is it this way? Because of *wrong believing*. Wrong believing gave birth to toil, to pain. Wrong believing was the reason sweat was necessary for victory. But God gave us a way to have sweatless victory without toil. It's the way of sowing a seed, in Jesus's mighty name, sowing for God to get the glory. Sowing because we believe God's Word.

God has given us a way to remove toil from our lives. A way to remove pain and suffering. A way to remove being forced to use our willpower. It's making the choice to use Word Power.

When we meditate on the Word, we are taking in His thoughts, and believing it on the inside. Once you believe it on the inside, the Word gives birth to behavior. Your way will become prosperous, and you will have good success.

The only good success is God's success because the only one good is God. Good success comes from good believing, right believing. Unfortunately, you can't bring success with right behavior alone. You can't say, *I'm going to read my Bible every day, go to every church service every Sunday.* Right behavior must spring forth from right beliefs. You must believe what God says about you; that Jesus saw you as valuable enough to die for, that you're a mighty man or woman of valor, who has something to offer, and a holy purpose.

If you begin to believe what God believes about you, you'll find you cannot help but say what God says about you. You'll say it on the inside, and you'll say it on the outside. Because right believing and right dreaming creates the right boundaries.

Right Boundaries

Right believing creates right boundaries. Right boundaries reveal enemies and cause right behaviors that make us able to contend with those enemies. God uses the victories over our enemies to boost our bold faith. Without boundaries, chaos reigns. Without boundaries, fear creeps in, and fear triumphs. We retreat into our caves, our ears unable to hear the resounding voice of God calling us to join the battle.

God wants us to believe right. By believing right, He can remove toil from our lives. He can take us from the place of toiling, sweating, and struggling to a place of peace, a place of victory. He wants us to morph from the guy working as hard as he can to the guy who rests while God does the work. He wants us to morph from the woman who thinks she can do it from her willpower to the woman who recognizes without God she is nothing. Then God can take us to a higher place, our highest ground.

If we pursue the right believing instead of high achieving, an amazing victory will be the result, without toil and sweat. The Spirit of God within moves us in the right way, into the fight of faith. Real, genuine, lasting change and metamorphosis only comes when we shed our limitations, come to peace with ourselves, and surrender to who God says we really are.

Ignoring right believing won't produce transformation. God cares about the thoughts and intents of our hearts. The thoughts and intents of the heart give us access to Jesus as our Savior. This gives God the opportunity to work in us and to take us to a place without struggle.

The Apostle Paul said:

> *When I was a child, I spake as a child, I understood as a child, I thought as a child: but when I became a man, I put away childish things.*
> (1 Corinthians 13:11, KJV)

Maturity from a child to a man doesn't come from age; it comes from thoughts and words. Our ability to rise—or fall—is in the power of our spoken thoughts.

Can you lay your old ego down on the altar? Can you believe you're forgiven when you don't see or feel like it? Can you say you're righteous when you feel sinful and dirty? Can you say, I am righteous because God made me righteous—not because of anything I've done, but because the Blood of Jesus made me clean?

Without the right believing, those words cannot be said. Only right belief in the Word of God and the blood of Jesus has the power to bring genuine change in our lives.

Our boundaries need to be built around rock-solid faith, positioned to produce for His glory. Boundaries help us endure, outlast, and outwit our opponent. They expose our times to fight, as well as the areas our enemies attack. Boundaries create safety, and safety facilitates rest. To completely avoid destruction, I've learned we need another vital thing as we're launched forward to the next part of our journey.

We need rest.

CHAPTER ELEVEN

• • • • • •

MAINTAINING REST AFTER THE
PROMISE IS POSSESSED

The world we currently live in has what I call a *microwave mentality*. When we have a microwave mentality, everything needs to be done fast—in a hurry. A microwave mentality doesn't care about the quality of the product as much as how quickly it can be heated up, spat out of the microwave, and consumed. But the truth is the best meals, the most mouth-watering meals, and the meals we celebrate the holidays with are meals that cannot be made in the microwave.

Why? They take *time.*

It takes time to produce excellence. It takes patience to construct something with love, to create a masterpiece.

That microwave mentality, while it does get things hot in a hurry, in the end, is dangerous, and destructive. The best things in life will always take patience and time.

We endure the sacrifice, the time necessary to create greatness because of our passion for the promise.

The Promise of Rest

One of the times I was incarcerated, one of the issues that arose in prison was about space—specifically, bed space for incoming prisoners.

After I had been locked up for five years, the state faced an overcrowding problem. Prison officials came up with the idea of shipping felons out of state, into Arizona and Minnesota, into their less-crowded prisons. Because of this, fear swept across the local penal institutions, knowing inmates would be upset and outraged at having to be shipped off to another state, away from their families.

How did they solve this? In the middle of the night, officers would knock on inmates' doors, enter their rooms, cuff them up, drag them out, chain them up, and ship them off on a plane out-of-state. Later, the officers put the missing inmates' clothes and personal possessions into boxes, which they set in front of their cell.

Next morning, guys on the block would wake and see boxes of their homeboy's belongings piled up, and know they'd been shipped to another state. This drove fear and anxiety to an all-time high. It became impossible to sleep, eat, and function in that environment. At any moment, someone could get a knock at the door and be carried off to another state bound in shackles.

During that fearful time, it was impossible to find rest. However, I had been meditating on a scripture that unlocked an understanding for me of how believing carries us into rest. The scripture was Hebrews 4:1–3 (KJV).

> *Let us therefore fear, lest, a promise being left us of entering into his rest, any of you should seem to come short of it. For unto us was the Gospel preached, as well as unto*

them: but the word preached did not profit
them, not being mixed with faith in them
that heard it. For we which have believed do
enter into rest, as he said, As I have sworn
in my wrath, if they shall enter into my rest:
although the works were finished from the
foundation of the world.

In these Hebrews verses, you'll notice that the things we believe must be mixed with faith. This means we empower them by acting as if we believe they are so. And when we act as if we believe what is preached, faith manifests these things in our life. It carries us into a place called rest.

Rest is transient. Rest isn't something you get—it's something you must maintain. So, rest will come and attempt to leave. You find rest as you meditate on God's promise, as you remember what God said He will perfect. You can find rest, or you can find stress, looking at the bills and the many overwhelming trials and troubles that come to pass in your life.

God enjoys performing the miraculous in the midst of rest. In fact, in the very beginning, it says God created the Heavens and the earth and mankind, and on the seventh day of creating He rested.

He didn't rest because He was tired—He rested because He was *finished*. Rest represents completion. When God completed the things He planned to do, He rested.

The moment the Word of God is believed in our heart, and we confess it with our mouth, conception takes place. The Word is conceived inside of us. We take possession of the Word, and as it develops, we need to maintain rest so that the Word can be manifested.

All through the Bible, you see miraculous events living at the address of rest. In Genesis 2:21, God gave Adam a wife when he was asleep. In Acts 12:6, Peter received the miracle of freedom while he slept. Mark, chapter 4, talks about a man sowing a seed and going to sleep night and day and awakening to a harvest. In the Gospels of Matthew through John, the miracles Jesus performed occurred on the Sabbath day, which means the day of rest.

Miracles are born inside of rest. In fact, Noah's name—as we learned before—means rest. Rest is where we possess our inheritance. Rest is where miracles manifest.

In a microwave society, we require things to happen fast. A microwave mentality doesn't require patience or permit rest. The Bible says in Hebrews 6:12:

> *That ye be not slothful, but followers of them who through faith and patience inherit the promises.*

Patience is necessary. We have to show God, ourselves, and the Devil that the promise we have possessed and have chosen to mix with our faith has given us rest. We're not anxious. We're not in fear. We're not overwhelmed with events and circumstances currently taking place.

Instead, we choose to be patient. We choose to stay single-minded in our faith. We choose to rest.

The Place Where Miracles Are Possessed

But how do you rest, without worrying that things will change without your control? When things in your life look bleak? When your rent's late, your car payments are overdue, and the unpaid bills are piling up?

I had six years left on a sentence when they began transferring inmates to Arizona and Minnesota. My thought-life overwhelmed me with dread, with the thought of going to sleep and being awakened in handcuffs, being dragged off in chains on a flight to another state.

One day, I saw my name on a list to meet with a counselor. I remember saying quietly on the inside, *God I trust you.* I needed to repeat that, over and over, to stop my quivering mind from panicking. But the moment I said, *God, I trust you,* it was as if warm honey poured from the inside of me, soothing and comforting me in the midst of my stress.

I went back to what Abraham did in Romans 4:19 (NKJV),

> *And not being weak in faith, he did not consider his own body, (since he was about a hundred years old), already dead, and the deadness of Sarah's womb.*

When Abraham thought about his wife Sarah, he thought that Sarah's physical ability to have children was dead because she was so old. However, God had given Abraham a promise that he would have a child. So Abraham, having received God's promise, had to intentionally command his thought-life so that he could rest and believe that God's promise would be so. He had to *not meditate* on it on purpose. He had to *not think* about all the things that were working against God's promise.

The way Abraham possessed rest was not only to mix his faith with what God said but to tell people God had promised he would one day conceive a child. He said it again, and again, and again. *I am Abraham. God has promised me a child.* He refused to think about or even consider the current circumstances, which spoke contrary to his spoken belief.

Any time Abraham meditated on the actual physical situation—his age (Abraham was over 100) and Sarah's barren womb—it depleted his faith and moved him away from rest. It caused him to fall into anxiety and fear. His momentary unbelief convinced him God's promise would never be possessed. So, Abraham fought to possess rest. Rest is important. Going back to Hebrews 4:9–11 (KJV),

> *There remaineth therefore a rest to the people of God. For he that is entered into his rest, he also hath ceased from his own works, as God did from his. Let us labour therefore to enter into that rest, lest any man fall after the same example of unbelief.*

What unbeliefs are those verses talking about? About the unbelief expressed in Hebrews 4:6, KJV,

> *Seeing therefore it remaineth that some must enter therein, and they to whom it was first preached entered not in because of unbelief.*

In Hebrews, the Israelites failed to receive God's promise because they failed to enter into rest. Fear continued to grow and breed in their lives because they considered circumstances. They meditated on what was against them, rather than what God said. Rest is the place where miracles are possessed. We must maintain rest.

When we maintain something, we possess momentum. If we try to push a car uphill, initially it takes an extreme amount of pressure against the obstacle of gravity to get the vehicle moving. But once we have it moving, it takes less pressure to *keep* it moving.

We maintain the pressure, so our momentum isn't broken. When we maintain rest, we maintain God's promises. When we maintain God's promises, we possess peace.

How do we step into our destiny? We apply pressure. We press past the downward pull. We show God we're accepting His upward call. *God, we trust you. God, we believe you.*

We speak it. We think it. We remind ourselves what God promised. We choose to refuse to consider anything other than God's restoration and renewal of our lives.

Choose to Refuse

I needed to choose to refuse.

In prison, everything served to remind me that I was a prisoner. Sure, I could walk around the penitentiary calling myself a free man—yet my every move was watched, documented, and controlled. Even the announcements over the loudspeaker told me when to rise, when to sleep, when I could spend an hour in the sunlight, and what hour I could eat.

Every second reminded me I was in bondage, that I was a highly violent prisoner. But instead of focusing on my current condition, I refused to think about it. Instead, I chose to think—*I'm free. I'm free from sin. I'm free from bad behavior. I'm free from everything I used to be, and I'm currently morphing from a natural man to a supernatural man. I'm currently morphing from a wicked man into a man of God.*

I maintained the pressure on my thought-life. Choosing to meditate on what God said about me, I possessed His promise. I became patient.

The Bible says, *"Let patience have her perfect work"* (James 1:4, KJV). Patience creates character. Patience brings change. Patience causes metamorphosis—it's what causes the caterpillar to take on wings.

Patience requires rest. Patience allows you to dream.

My mentality was…meditate on what God says, regardless of what I can see, so the Word of God can work in me. I knew that if I turned the pressure off, I would not only lose momentum but eventually, the things that could be seen would apply so much pressure on me that they would run me over. And then I would fall into self-defeating thoughts, into believing the lies of the enemy and fail to enter the promise because of my unbelief.

I chose to maintain rest after the promise was possessed, as I chose to keep the pressure on and press to the high calling of Christ Jesus, momentum was gained. As I gained momentum, it took less pressure to maintain rest. Over time, I came to a place where I could simply dream and take joy from the dream. In fact, I could borrow joy from tomorrow in the midst of a dream.

While I was inside the razor wires, I asked my wife to send me pictures of the stairwell at my house, the kids' bedroom, the bathroom, and pictures of the car in the driveway. What was I doing? *I was receiving building blocks for my dream.*

I put the pictures on the bunk above me. As I lay in bed, I would look up at the pictures and meditate, seeing myself running up the stairs after my children. I would see myself entering my child's bedroom and reading Bible stories to them. I would see myself climbing into the car to take my children to school. I would see myself spending time with my wife at our dining room table, talking about the day's events.

What was I doing? *I was laboring to enter rest.*

When the Word says *labor into rest,* it's not talking about hard toil—it's talking about *believing* (Hebrews 4:11). Remember, it's the right believing that creates the miraculous, not high achieving. So, simply using my imagination and speaking out loud thanksgiving to God because I believed it was so, I rejoiced and took joy from the photos I saw.

That labor created the building blocks for my dream. That labor maintained rest. That gave me the ability to sleep when everybody else was filled with stress and fear because they imagined they'd be shipped out at any time.

During that season, I recall guys coming up to me and saying, "Free Man, how is it you're not upset or panicking about this shipment they're doing of people in the middle of the night?"

"I don't have anything to fear," I responded. "I trust God."

I had reasons to be afraid in the natural, the same as these men. Afraid that I may lose my wife or lose my children. But I chose to possess rest, to maintain rest, and while lots of other people were shipped out around me, I stayed and rested.

If you will maintain rest after the promise is possessed, the promise you confessed will manifest. Once the promise is conceived, the promise grows inside of you. As it grows, the image you perceive on the inside grows.

The promise made it easier for me to take joy from tomorrow when events were going on around me that could cause sorrow. It made it easier for patience to have its perfect work while I was maintaining faith in the promise.

Rest in the Promise

Rest is where the promise is possessed.

Rest is where we gain our inheritance.

We labor to enter rest. We believe with our hearts, confess with our mouths, act as if it is so, then continue to rejoice and give God thanksgiving, even when everything around us tells us it is not so. We choose on purpose not to consider these things because we believe God regardless of what we see.

As we undergo metamorphosis, we arrive at the place where the only required evidence that a promise is so, is the promise itself.

Once we arrive at that place, we find peace. We experience rest. We choose to refuse to check our flesh to see if the promise really happened—to check our bank account to see if the money is there or to stare at our phone after a job interview, anxiously watching for that new employer to call. We refuse to consider those who say that God is a liar and choose to rejoice because we've found freeing affirmation in the Word of God.

Then we not only possess rest, but we possess the promise that will manifest itself again and again and again. We experience change on the outside and change from within.

Rest and momentum are the things God used to change me.

Three key elements also had to be maintained for me to maintain rest. Those three elements were:

> *Forgiving.*
> *Forgetting.*
> And *never quitting.*

God instructed me in each of these things, equipping me to be the catalyst for change in my own life, developing empowering habits to battle the lies I heard in my head. By *forgiving, forgetting, and never quitting,* I kicked the enemy's internal voice out of my head and affirmed the eternal truth about who God said I really was.

CHAPTER TWELVE

• • ● • •

FORGIVING, FORGETTING, AND NEVER QUITTING

I wasted years hating myself, hating my behaviors, and hating my world, locked in a cage of unforgiveness. Did my anger and self-hatred change anything? It did not. Instead, my unforgiveness like a thief stole from me and robbed me. I went through life believing my anger was justified, hindered by my past pain until all that anger became a heavy burden buried deep in my soul.

That burden became my bondage. My unforgiveness bore poisonous fruit. Attacking my vulnerability, Satan hindered me from following God's Will. I wasted years this way, unable to press forward. Alone in my secret place one day, I read this scripture in 1 Corinthians 9:24 (KJV):

> *Know ye not that they which run in a race run all, but one receiveth the prize? So run, that ye may obtain.*

In my mind, I puzzled that last part out; *Run the race to win.* What exactly was that part of the verse talking about?

The word *run* brought me back to when I was a freshman in high school.

I ran track. I remember running the 800, and at the start of the second lap, I'd feel my body grow heavier, the distance to the finish line grow farther, and the oxygen in my lungs become thinner. The pressure to give up the race grew more and more powerful. As my feet pounded the track and my heart hammered in my chest, I realized the nearer I came to the finish line, the more pressure there was. The nearer I came to the prize, the greater my fear became that I'd fail to finish the race.

The moment I read the verse in Corinthians, a switch flipped inside of me. Having an unlimited amount of time in my cell, I checked out Strong's Concordance, searching everywhere it mentioned the word *run*, just to see if it could explain to me what "to run" meant. I was led to Galatians 5:7 (NKJV), which says:

> *You ran well. Who hindered you from obeying the truth?*

That told me that the 1 Corinthians verse was about the run of obeying the truth. There are things that will hinder us from continuing to run. The Bible tells us that "we walk by faith, not by sight" (2 Corinthians 5:7, NKJV). The walk of faith means going from faith to faith, putting my left foot out, then my right foot. To keep my equilibrium balanced I step left, then right, placing all of my weight one step at a time out in front of me...

Stepping *in faith.*

God says when we're walking by faith, and we consistently walk by faith, we're walking in the truth. We love people, we give, and we obey God's truth. In our faith walk, we build momentum until finally, we come to the place where we build our momentum into a run. At the same time, forces will attempt to hinder us, as we attempt to run. Sometimes what hinders us from running will be in the form of people. People's ideas, their words, their thoughts, will poison our minds and hinder us from forgiving others for their injustices.

Hebrews 12:1 (KJV) explains clearly what we need to do, to press past old mistakes and failures, and develop the persistence it takes to keep running. It says,

> *Wherefore seeing we also are compassed about with so great a cloud of witnesses, let us lay aside every weight, and the sin which doth so easily beset us, and let us run with patience the race that is set before us.*

The Weight and Patience

Patience. My eyes teared up, the first time I read that verse. I wanted to act now, not wait for change.

But God has a process for everything. We can't prosper in life with a microwave mentality or a wishy-washy mindset. If we're to run in such a way as to win the race, it's by driving fear out by diving in and leading the battle.

Hebrews, chapter 12, says to lay aside every weight. Weights create additional pressure on our run. If I weigh 300 pounds, it's going to be a lot harder for me to win the race than if I weigh 150 pounds.

The weight that Hebrews, chapter 12, is talking about is different. It's the weight of things we have taken on in our lives. Once we take them on, they begin to press us down, to shackle us with weight, to become oppressive. Whether it's bitterness, anger, or sin, it besets our run and hinders our ability to win.

Think about the word *beset*. Beset means you're encircled or surrounded by some force, which causes you to cease moving forward. Instead of creating forward momentum, that force becomes an obstacle, a hurdle, forcing you to run around it. As you navigate around it you bump into another obstacle, then another, and another until you are forced to stop, encircled by all these stumbling blocks.

Weight creates a burden. Weight creates unnecessary strain.

As I meditated on the word *weight*, God reminded me of the importance of forgiving, and forgetting. There are elements of weight involved in both.

When it comes to forgiving, we're releasing a weight. When we forgive, it's because we have been offended. After being offended, we desire to remove the weight of the offense, so it doesn't hinder our run. So, it cannot choke out what the Word of God is attempting to grow inside of us. But it's not just forgiving of other people who have hindered us—we also must learn to forgive ourselves. Being unforgiving of ourselves becomes another weight, another unnecessary burden we choose to carry.

Because we live in a world where trouble and hostility and conflict are present, the opportunity to practice forgiveness is going to appear almost every day. Scripture makes it crystal clear how to deal with our troubles. In the Gospels, Jesus tells us, "...Let not your heart be troubled. Neither let it be afraid" (John 14:27, KJV).

The truth of Jesus's words really hits home. Stop giving yourself permission to be troubled. Stop giving permission to fear to enter in.

Why is Jesus saying not to give it permission? Because nothing can change your condition without your permission.

If you refuse to let offense remain in your life, it can't weigh you down.

Learn to forgive quickly.

When we forgive quickly, we launch ourselves forward on our race. But if we aren't ready to forgive, God can't launch our feet at a winning speed, in a winning direction. It takes time. All change takes time. Patience allows purpose to take root. Purpose brings healing.

Increase sometimes occurs in small amounts. The Bible says that one sows and another waters, but God gives the increase (1 Corinthians 3:7). You won't be able to forgive everybody immediately when you first start. Some struggles take longer. It was harder for me to forgive myself than it was to forgive others. I'd been walking around with the weight of me all my life and walking with the weight of other people only for a season.

But I was ready to run. I knew God was leading me somewhere. And going somewhere, I couldn't carry around the weight of bitterness, unforgiveness, or resentment. So, I made sure to do three important things:

> *Forgive.*
> *Forgive quickly.*
> And *never stop forgiving.*

Through Christ, we're all forgiven. Allow that spirit of forgiveness to penetrate you and turn you into a forgiver—a forgiver who forgives quickly and forgives forever. Or suffer the consequences. The moment we choose not to forgive, we take on agonizing weight. Eventually, that agonizing weight will overload us, and we'll be dragging around anger, bitterness, offense, and outrage until we stumble into a pit.

Shake that weight off now. Don't be held down by some old offense. Our ability to run our race well relies on the power of forgiveness.

Pedal-to-the-Metal Potential

The Holy Spirit often talks to me in rhymes. I believe that's because back in the day, I was a rapper. Since I was a rapper, I focus and meditate on rhymes—it makes things easier for me to remember.

One little rhyme came to me as I was teaching. In the middle of my message, I heard this internal rhyme in my mind: *Condemnation is the glue—That the curse sticks to.*

That rhyme explained something to me. You see, condemnation is the definition of unforgiveness. So, *"Condemnation is the glue—That the curse sticks to,"* spoke to me of a warning. The enemy wants to get us to the place where we will condemn others and ourselves. When we condemn, we magnetize ourselves to the enemy's curse.

However, because I am redeemed, forgiven, and shown mercy by the love of Jesus and the sacrifice of Jesus, this makes it easier for me to turn away from condemning anyone. I choose to refuse to hold offense. I don't care what that offense is—I choose to refuse.

But forgetting? How does one forget?

There are two things God wants us to forget. He wants us to forget the things we've done wrong in our past. And He wants us to forget the things we've done right in our past.

That sounds strange, doesn't it? Still, God wants us to forget the bad stuff because He doesn't want you to have a consciousness of sin. And He wants us to forget our good successes because He wants us to press for a higher calling, to keep climbing to the top. He wants us to press into the next level.

What often happens is that once people forget about their sin, they forget about the pain of the past and become immobile, inactive, stagnant. They reach a successful place and decide to stay there. They don't recognize that by ceasing to press upward they've stopped their increase. They've shut off the flow of the even greater things God wants them to possess.

Stagnation—the lack of movement—is the beginning stage of death. Increasing is the characteristic heart of God. The very first words that ever penetrated an eardrum were the words, "be blessed, be fruitful and multiply" (Genesis 1:28). Those were the first words that ever vibrated through the sky into the eardrums of a man—a blessing of *increase.*

But, the mentality that says, *I'm good, I'm successful, I'm going to settle right here* is also the mentality that says, *I'm going to rebel against what God said. I'm going to stop because I'm happy with where I am.*

Don't become fixated upon where you are. Stagnation is crippling. Stagnation makes you feeble. Put the pedal-to-the-metal when it comes to your potential.

Release Increase

Life is all about change. If you choose to refuse to remain stagnant, by God's power, you'll continue to grow.

As you choose to forget about the pain of the past and your current success, progress becomes easy. You choose to look with the eyes and the lens of wisdom into the future, where God wants to lead you. That's the mentality that says, *I'm not going to allow the weight of unforgiveness to hold me down and stop me. I'm not going to stop and stand still, and let sin surround me. I'm going to continue to run.*

Continue to run, in such a way that you win the race. Never stop pressing to the next level. Never stop pressing toward God's "next" in your life. Don't stop the process. God's process of increase does not end. God will continue to release increase forever. Choose to run in such a way that you continue to possess increase forever.

Now, I don't mean to say that gain is Godliness. Just because you receive something better than you had yesterday doesn't mean you are closer to God. But the more you get to know about God and surrender to God, the more your pursuit of increase will grow.

— You will have an increased impact on the world around you.
— You will want to increase God's blessing everywhere the curse resides.
— You will want to increase light everywhere darkness reigns.
— You will want to increase peace everywhere there is chaos.
— You will want to increase comfort everywhere there is pain.
— You will want to increase laughter everywhere there are tears.
— You will want to increase abundance everywhere there is lack.

Why? Because God's love has no end. Why? Because God has infinite power and wants a heart relationship with each of us. Why? Because now you're running in such a way that God wins the battle *through you.*

If you remain stagnant, you refuse to be a blessing in the earth. If you stand still and settle, rather than pressing onward, you die to His possibilities and His promises and suffer death to the world around you.

But once you press upward from less than enough to more than enough, you can be used by God to bring hope, inspiration, and encouragement to others. As a result, the love of God can be spread across the earth. By releasing the love of God and turning off the effects of pain and suffering, we are implementing Godly change in the world around us.

Forgiving yourself is impactful. Forgiving others is crucial. Forgetting about what you did wrong as well as forgetting what you did right is critical. Refusing to surrender and refusing to quit means admitting there's another higher level that you have not yet obtained.

This is so that God can get more glory from your story. Run the race. Run again and again, and run to win. Never stop pursuing the next level in God. Never stop pursuing the next level in intimacy and relationship with Him. Never stop pursuing the next level of impact that He can have in the world around you. Never stop pursuing the next level of influence He'll give you as He enlarges your territory and blesses you indeed.

Never stop. Why? Because God never stops. Our God is a consuming fire. Because He lives lit and His fire can never go out, we also should live lit and never go out.

If there's something higher, we too must burn for it like a never-ending fire.

Forgive quickly. Forgive others. Forgive yourself. And then forget quickly. Forget your mistakes as well as your successes as you press onward to possess what God has for you next.

CHAPTER THIRTEEN

• • • ● • • •

HIGHER HEIGHT FROM HIGHER SIGHT

Recently, I attended an international faith conference in Chicago. At the completion of the evening service, hungry and needing to grab a bite to eat, we decided to head downtown and visit a restaurant on the ninety-sixth floor of one of the city's tallest buildings. As we parked on the street, our vehicle faced a dimly lit alley. When I opened my car door and gazed across the dark street, my stomach dropped, and I froze.

Wobbling across the street was a gigantic hairy rat, the size of a small raccoon or a housecat. Usually, rats run full speed and disappear into the shadows. This rat strutted right out of the alleyway and cruised up the crosswalk as if he'd decided to take a nighttime stroll and was warning everybody; *This is* my *neighborhood.* Soon as he hit the curb the rat waddled sideways, licking his slobbery lips like he'd just climbed out of a garbage can and disappeared down into the sewer.

I watched the rat, my stomach turning, disgusted. It was like sirens started screaming inside my skull. The sight of it spoke of everything negative in the city—dead things, decay, disease, and the defiled. But as I locked my car and entered the building, climbed ninety-six floors to the very top of the restaurant and looked out the windows, I suddenly experienced a different view. I no longer saw the defiled and dirty things crawling around in the gutter. Instead, I could see to the far horizons, across the city from the high-rise sky-scrapers to the glittering nightclubs and the sports stadiums, all the way across the Illinois state line. My view was no longer limited to this one dark street. My view was of the world in its entirety.

This view marked a lasting memory of beauty beyond what I had seen before. I had vacillated from ugly to beauty only moments apart. Within minutes, I experienced a renewed view.

Renewed View

2 Kings, chapter, 6 tells the story about Elisha and the king of Syria. The king has attacked Israel, lost his troops in an ambush, and is intensely angry. So angry, in fact, that he suspects somebody in his camp is actually a spy for his enemy.

Suspecting there's a snitch in his midst, the king goes to his servant for some inside information. His servant tells the king there are no spies. "But," the servant says, there is a man of God in Israel named Elisha, who hears and "tells the king of Israel the words that you speak in your bedroom" (2 Kings 6:12, NKJV).

Enraged, the king of Syria sends an army to seek out and find this man of God who knows what he says in his bedroom, who causes his armies to be defeated.

Beginning in 2 Kings 6:14 (KJV), the story continues:

Therefore sent he thither horses and chariots and a great host: and they came by night, and compassed the city about. And when the servant of the man of God was risen early, and gone forth, behold, a host compassed the city both with horses and chariots. And His servant said unto him, "Alas, my master! how shall we do?" And he answered, "Fear not: for they that be with us are more than they that be with them." And Elisha prayed and said, "Lord, I pray thee, open his eyes, that he may see." And the Lord opened the eyes of the young man; and he saw: and, behold, the mountain was full of horses and chariots of fire round about Elisha. And when they came down to him, Elisha prayed unto the Lord, and said, "Smite this people, I pray thee, with blindness." And he smote them with blindness according to the word of Elisha. And Elisha said unto them, "This is not the way, neither is this the city: follow me, and I will bring you to the man whom you seek." But he led them to Samaria. And it came to pass, when they were come into Samaria, that Elisha said, "Lord, open the eyes of the men, that they may see." And the Lord opened their eyes, and they saw; and, behold, they were in the midst of Samaria. And the King of Israel, said unto Elisha, when he saw them, "My father, shall I smite them? shall I smite them?" And he answered, "Thou shalt not smite them: wouldest thou smite those whom thou has taken captive with thy sword and with thy bow? set bread and water before them, that they may eat and drink, and go to their master." And he prepared great provision for them: and when they had eaten and drunk, he sent them away, and they went to their master. So the bands of Syria came no more into the land of Israel.

Elisha's story is about having a renewed view. Elisha received a *higher sight from a higher height.* Elisha had a supernatural relationship with God, to the degree that he could hear the conversations of his enemies, and prevent catastrophe from falling upon the people of God.

Elisha had a higher view than the people in his midst. When the armies of Syria arrived to attack Elisha, his servant looking out exclaimed that the armies had Elisha surrounded, that they were more than his master could handle, that death and doom were guaranteed. But Elisha sees from a higher level. Elisha looked out, saw the Syrian army, but also saw that the army of God was in their midst. He prayed to God to open the eyes of his servant and lifting open his eyes his servant witnessed chariots of fire.

When God opened the servant's eyes, he saw with the eyes of the Holy Spirit. God allowed Elisha's servant to see who was with him, who was for him, and who was there to fight the battle. This calmed Elisha's servant and eliminated all his fears. It gave the servant confidence to go down with Elisha and face the armies that stood before him.

Defective Perspective

It's amazing how a single view from a higher height can change the way you think about your current condition. It's amazing how a view beyond the normal can make normal things have no value. It can make normal things have no impact, no effect on us in any negative way.

Elisha's servant—like myself high above the streets of Chicago—saw beyond the small things, which look bad right in front of him. When I was on the top of the skyscraper, looking off into the distance beyond state lines, I remember thinking to myself that every single light of the hundreds of thousands of lights I could see represented a room with people. Immediately this made me picture the enormous number of people within that area. I pictured the enormous potential in each of these people. I thought about the difference between the state I was standing in and the state I could see looking across the darkness.

This is how a different view can affect you. You can view things with awe and wonder, with a reverential potential or a defective perspective.

In the story of Elisha, God turned the view of His servant to see heavenly things rather than earthly things. When Elisha went down into the midst of the enemy army, the Bible says that God blinded them, so the enemy couldn't see that the person they were talking to was the enemy they had pursued to destroy.

Afterward, Elisha led them into the Samarian camp—the camp of their enemies—to become captives. While they were walking with Elisha, they were blind to the fact that their pursuit had landed them into the hands of their enemies.

When they arrived in Samaria, God opened their eyes—and at that moment, they knew they were dead men. But Elisha had mercy. He fed them, and sent them away, to report back to the king of Syria that there was no possible way to defeat the people of God, so long as there was a man amongst them who could see from a higher height and have a higher sight than they had.

That kind of higher vision creates calm. In calm, we find commitment.

Think about the ability to create commitment.

Think about the ability to encourage or discourage.

These things are within view if we allow God to open our eyes to them.

The visible realm is limited. Your vision is limited. It's limited in scope depending on where it's coming from.

When I was a little boy—and I was a small child, under four feet tall—my mom's house seemed huge to me. In fact, there were areas I couldn't even see. But as I grew, I began to see things from a different angle. And as I rose up in my height, the same house that once seemed huge became small to me.

It wasn't the size of the house that changed. It was *me.*

My perspective changed.

When we grab hold of the Word of God and the things of God, our perspective changes—we're no longer limited by the things we can see. When it's dark, we barely see what's right in front of us. When it's light and we're in a high place, visibility allows us to see far off.

The Bible talks about wisdom as being the ability to see afar off. The Bible talks about the wisdom of God as the ability to have a higher level of sight and vision. Perhaps no greater example of this is in the story of Solomon, who offered an immense sacrifice to God, then asked God for wisdom. God granted Solomon's wish. And as a result of wisdom, Solomon could see things far beyond the natural realm.

Higher Height of Sight

Your perspective will always affect the way you respond to your current condition. If I can see what God sees, I'll respond the way God responds. But if I can only see what men see, I'll respond like a mortal man—penetrated by fear, insecurity, anxiety.

A higher height of sight comes from the Word of God. In Isaiah 55:8–11 (KJV), God tells us:

> *"For my thoughts are not your thoughts, neither are your ways, my ways," saith the Lord. "For as the heavens are higher than the earth, so are my ways higher than your ways, and my thoughts than your thoughts. For as the rain comes down, and the snow from heaven, and returns not thither, but waters the earth, and makes it bring forth and bud, that it may give seed to the sower, and bread to the eater. So shall my word be that goes forth out of my mouth: it shall not return unto me void, but it shall accomplish that which I please, and it shall prosper in the thing whereto I sent it."*

There is a higher way of thinking. A higher way of doing things. A higher way of seeing things. And that way is God's way. In pursuit of higher heights and higher thoughts, we must first pursue what God thinks about us.

In prison, I read the story of Moses and how Moses killed a man and buried him in the sand. As I read that story, I thought to myself, *Man, in Washington State, Moses would've gotten first-degree aggravated murder charges, and he would've been electrocuted! But God saw Moses as a man after his own heart!*

Look at the Apostle Paul. Paul was a man who persecuted Christians and stoned them to death. Normally, that type of contentious individual would be hunted down and killed by his enemies—yet God used him to write a large portion of His Bible.

David was a man so moved by lust that he went after a woman, Bathsheba, stole her as his wife and killed her husband, so he could have her. This is one of the worst, vilest acts imaginable! A sex offense. Lust led David to violence—yet the Bible says God called David a man after his own heart.

Why did God utilize men who had done such evil things? Because God has a *higher sight,* He sees beyond our current condition, into our potential. He sees His plan bearing fruit in our lives.

As I meditated on these three individuals as well as Elisha, I concluded that God could forgive any of us—not only because He loved us, and He wanted to restore the right relationship with us, but also because He understands the potential He put in us.

His sight of us will always be beyond what we can see of ourselves.

My opinions were shaped by the things I had seen visibly. My opinion of myself was formed from external elements—thugs, guns, drugs—in the world around me. But once I turned away from what I could see visibly and turned toward what God calls revelation knowledge, I climbed from the low level of external information to the high level of Godly revelation. Once I reached that higher level, I could see as the eagle sees, and in the midst of a storm I could climb above it, and see far beyond it.

I could make a willful decision to pursue God's thoughts in the midst of circumstances that were attempting to force bad thoughts into me. I could see beyond those circumstances into what God sees and change the amount of power I had accessible to me in those times.

Elisha and his servant could see what God showed them. They could make a demand on God's presence and change the circumstances they were trapped in. The Word of God has the ability to filter out our most debilitating thoughts: insecurity, fear, condemnation. That filter is the word of love, which is God, Himself, who is love, causing us to look through the lens of love, and to see things differently than we saw them in the absence of love.

In love, we see ourselves as valuable. We see other people as valuable. No matter how evil, how violent, how wicked or how perverse we have been, being restored to a right relationship with God can penetrate all that perversity, all of that evil, all of that wickedness, and transform us to a masterpiece of His creation.

A higher sight from a higher height makes trouble seem tiny. In fact, the higher you go, and the further down you look at things—like a rat crossing a big city street—the tinier they become. When we choose to refuse to look at low-level living and instead look at the bigger picture and how God can use us to overcome any trouble that arises, no matter how big, how small, our troubles become like small pebbles in the road. They become grains of sand we can simply step over, as we press to possess God's success and His plan for our lives.

Innervisions

Vision from a higher height determines how high we're willing to reach, how far we're willing to go, to reach our destiny. If our vision is from a low place, obstacles and hurdles look huge and insurmountable. But when our vision rises to a high place, obstacles become pebbles, if not sand, in our midst.

What's necessary is a vision change. Just think about the way God created our eyes. The reason we have two eyes is to see our world in stereo. Stereo sight gives us depth perception, which helps our brain decipher distance. God's purpose in giving us two eyes was to see in-depth because He planned on showing us things afar off in the distance. As a result, we'd be willing to press forward and pursue the thing we could see far off.

The same is true spiritually.

When God gives us a vision of a high place, our internal depth perception changes our attitude and our countenance, and enables us to endure until we possess the power God's given us to transform our lives.

We need to have the right vision.

A God vision.

And a high vision.

Higher height from higher sight enables us to walk in audacious faith. If the vision for your life isn't big enough, God can't do the impossible in your life. Vision is that vital building block, in building and deepening your relationship with God.

CHAPTER FOURTEEN

VISION AS THE CREATOR OF CHANGE

Back in the day, photographic images were created in a much different way than they are today. The film would be placed inside a camera. A shutter would open, flashing light through the lens onto the film, exposing it to the light. Then the negative inside the camera would be removed and taken through a chemical process in a dark room so that whatever the film was exposed to could be developed. After the negative was developed, it could be printed onto paper and reveal, in a perfect image, what the light had exposed.

This is the same way we are changed.

We are changed by being exposed to a completely new image. Something we had not originally seen.

In 2 Corinthians 5:17 (KJV), it says,

> *Therefore, if any man be in Christ he is a new creature: old things are passed away; behold, all things are become new.*

The biggest revelation in that scripture isn't the promise that we've become brand new, by being in Christ Jesus. The biggest revelation is *how* we become brand new. That revelation is inside of the word *behold*. Again, it says: "*Therefore, if any man be in Christ he is a new creature: old things are passed away; behold, all things are become new*" (2 Corinthians 5:17, KJV).

Why is *behold* right there? The dictionary defines *behold* as to "see or observe (a thing or person, especially a remarkable or impressive one)" ("Behold" 2019).

The Bible says *behold* because we need to take a long look and be exposed to the glory of the brand new.

Just as the original image had to enter our camera and be taken into the darkroom to be developed, just as the superhero had to enter a secret place so he or she could change, just as the caterpillar had to climb into the darkness of the cocoon to struggle and be completely transformed through metamorphosis, we too are changed by the method of *beholding*.

In fact, the word *behold* is in the Bible 212 times. Two hundred twelve times we're told by God's Word to *behold*. We're instructed to see, consider, meditate, imagine, and wholeheartedly be exposed to the glory of the kingdom of Heaven, and to behold that we are God's chosen instrument of change.

A Clearer Mirror

Another scripture in the Bible explains this concept more clearly. It's found in 2 Corinthians 3:18:

> *But we all, with an open face beholding as in a glass the glory of the Lord, are changed into the same image from glory to glory, even as by the Spirit of the Lord.*

The words *"beholding as in a glass"* tell us we're gazing into a mirror. By beholding God's Word, we're pushing closer to a looking glass, making certain the image we see reflected is of a Spirit-filled overcomer. But notice those two words right before beholding: the verse says, *"open face"*. Here, *open face* means to have removed the cover, to take the lid off the heart of man so that the heart can be exposed. To have an *open face* means to be open and ready to receive. It means to be open to complete change.

In the same scripture, 2 Corinthians 3:18, *beholding with open face* means to receive by repetition, compounded by intensity. By receiving repetitions we compound the Word of God, making it more intense inside of us. As a result, the Word changes us into what we see.

It's identical to the way film develops into an image, by going into a dark room. That dark place represents the inner portion of us, the hidden place of the heart, the hidden heart of man. Going into that darkened place and having the heart exposed to the Word by repetition, changes us from the inside out.

When the Bible tells us we are changed into the same image from glory to glory, it means we're changed from level to level. In other words, the amount of intensity we focus on meditating determines the outcome. The outcome is a result of the input.

Why does God want us to behold? Because our vision determines what we change into. The thing we see we will eventually believe. As a result of believing, we will eventually behave, according to what we've seen. That behavior becomes a habit, the habit becomes character, and character leads to destiny.

We need to intentionally and with purpose *behold*. This is how I was changed from a criminal and convicted killer, into a servant of Christ and His follower. After years of input, I possessed the love of God inside of me. God's love made me want to help the hurting, rather than hurt the hurting. As a result of in-depth, intense repetition and compounded intensity of open-faced beholding of the Word of God—as if I were gazing into a mirror—I discovered Christ could be formed in me, and I too could go from the lowly view of the caterpillar to the higher view of God's plan. And there, I could see what God saw about me.

Acclimate and Meditate

Joshua, chapter 1, holds another definition of the beholding process. Let's look at verse 8:

> *This book of the law, shall not depart out of thy mouth; but thou shalt meditate therein day and night...*

The word *meditate* means to mutter, to speak it out loud, then to paint a picture on the inside of your mind. First, we meditate on the Word, and then we observe to do what's written therein. We see ourselves walking the Word out, just as Jesus and His disciples did. And through our walk, the Word is released and revealed through us into today's society.

When we meditate on the Word day and night, we observe to do according to what we see written in the Word. We observe ourselves doing it and doing it until the compounded repetition changes our mindset. And when it changes a mindset, it changes a result.

Think of an old-fashioned alarm clock—the kind you wound and set to the time you wanted the alarm to ring. When the hands on the clock lined up with the hands of the alarm setting, the clock would scream. The alarm setting guaranteed that the behavior of the clock would be set in the right place.

This happens with us when we behold God's Word. We begin to change to match our settings. We begin to change what alarms us. As a result, we respond differently when our internal alarm goes off because our default settings have been changed.

Succumb to Become, Aim to Became

Meditating day and night doubles the compounded interest of our prayers, the relentless rhythm of our praying becomes the rock-solid backbeat of our life.

For instance, if every morning, I remind myself of His word in my life by speaking aloud, "I am in Jesus and in me is wisdom, righteousness, sanctification, and redemption." And every night I say aloud, "Jesus is in me, and I have wisdom, righteousness, sanctification, and redemption," those night and day repetitions compound the intensity of what I believe. It creates a powerful image of myself being wise. It creates a positive picture of myself being the redeemed, being the righteous, being sanctified unto God. Those images begin to affect my behaviors because they change the settings in my heart.

Joshua 1:8 says that by beholding, by meditating, by saying and seeing what the Word of God says—not only as a mirror but as a positioning—I can become a new creature in Christ Jesus. Seeing forces change in the life of the beholder. In fact, vision reveals depth, and depth provides room for the decision of pursuit or the absence of pursuit.

If I'm standing on a hill and I see a Walmart afar off, if my appetite is big enough it'll drive me to take the journey to possess what I want. My vision helps me to decide if my journey is worth the trip or not. Once I decide to take the trip, I begin the process—like the caterpillar—of metamorphosis. I change from being the person in one position to the person in a new position and a new place.

All of God's grace is led to us from glory to glory. It's taking us from one place to the next place.

If you are changing, wherever you are now is not where you will be. If you're a believer, your level will be higher in the days to come. Beholding is the effective release of the power that is within what you behold.

You behold, then you become what you beheld. You become what you became when you believed.

Now that sounds strange, to become what you already became.

But the moment you become in Christ, according to 2 Corinthians 5:17, you become brand new. The new portion of you is in your hidden heart. The supernatural power of God is within the hidden place. The only way to access that hidden supernatural power within is to get our soul and mind settings changed. Once they're re-set to what God already says about us, we'll behold His Scriptures and see the bridge He created to carry us to our divine purpose.

Believe and Declare

We were meant to see and become what we've seen.

We were meant to meditate, mutter, speak, and hear what God is whispering to us.

We were created to believe by beholding.

We were created to not only believe in our hearts but then to confess with our mouths what we believe in our hearts. A confession that comes from our mouths compounds our intense belief, and because it's been spoken it has the power to penetrate and affect the world around us.

We then begin to believe and declare. And we repeat the process.

Believe and declare.

Believe and declare.

The more we declare, the more we see ourselves wearing the Word, and walking in the Word. We see ourselves experiencing the same almighty power Jesus's disciples experienced. We refuse to allow distractions to distance us from the right actions. Instead, we focus our attention to beholding what God says about us.

Within us, metamorphosis then takes place. We discover there is power resident within us, power we can tap into, again and again, power residing in God's truth.

Believing starts with beholding. Exposure is the answer.

The question then arises as to what we've been exposed to.

If we've been exposing the film of our heart to the images of the world—the hateful, negative images we see in social media, the images we behold on television, movies, and in certain types of music—our beliefs create behaviors that open the door for the same negative outcomes. If we are filled with bitterness and speak of our offense to others, we transfer the bitterness into their hearts. Soon, they behave the way we do and share that bitterness with others.

But if we choose to behold what God says, to see what God says for us to see, to behold with an open face the Word of God as if it's a mirror showing our true image, it will change us. Without effort, we'll wake to discover one day we are completely different.

In my life, there are those who struggle to believe the story of the evil man I once was. It's because I tell that story from a changed position that makes it seem as if it was a lie.

And it *was* when I lived it.

The man I now am—the way I think, the way I speak, the way I act—paints a portrait of a man completely different, completely opposite to that individual. It's a result of meditating day and night on the awesome promises of God and observing myself doing all that was written therein. As a result, God lifted me out of the pit, made my way prosperous, and gave me good success.

You see, the only effort necessary for us to enter metamorphosis, to morph from the caterpillar into the butterfly, from the natural man into the supernatural man, is *to believe and to behold.*

Say and see what God said.

If we'll do that, absolute change will come. We will become who and what God says we're created to be. We will experience the revelation that our spirit has complete control of our flesh because our soul has come into agreement with God. We will no longer have an internal argument.

The Glory within Your Story

This book is my story.

This is what God did in my life.

He showed me I was in warfare—my internal battle zone. My life was His battlefield. God was fighting on my behalf, for all He had promised me. All I needed to do was take a risk, see His light instead of the dark, believe in His truth, and claim my freedom.

— This is why God planted in me the need to understand that my current identity was brought about by the negative lies I believed in my mind about myself.

— This is why He had to show me that my identity brought on adversity.

— This is why it was necessary for me to enter the secret place, so He could show me the fixes that were necessary.

— This is why He showed me the rejection connection, so I could disconnect from the pain of having been rejected.

God knew it would be necessary for me to learn to become comfortable with being uncomfortable while I changed.

— He knew there was an enemy in inner me, stopping Him from releasing the true purpose He had placed in me.

— He needed me to pursue the root so I could uproot those issues that were attempting to keep me bound in wrong behaviors.

— He wanted me to learn that right believing was necessary, and not high achieving because right believing would cause me to possess success where in the past wrong believing had created failure.

— He taught me about maintaining rest. How important it was to forgive and to forget, and to never give up in forgiving, forgetting, and pressing towards possessing the high calling He created me to walk in.

— He raised my view and my depth perception of who I really am. Beholding that vision became the creator of change in me.

That's my story.
Now it's your turn.

While you've been reading this book, not only have areas in your life been revealed where God is working to morph you but while reading these words God has been pouring in His healing power to bring about that change.

The metamorphosis process has begun.

It will take you from a low place, into the high place of His grace.

You see, God is not only in the business of morphing convicted criminals and killers into Christ-following individuals—He's in the business of changing everyone who will behold Him and believe what He says as if it is so.

You came to these pages, not by accident. I believe you came to this book with a purpose—the purpose of God, reminding you of who He made you to be. God's plan for you is beyond anything you have imagined. This story—my story—is the story of everyone: the story of complete change and continuous change. It was instrumental that you picked up my story so that God can reveal His glory from within *your* story.

We are all important to God. If God took the time to speak to a criminal, a gang leader, a drug dealer, and a killer, He will do the same for you.

He will empower you to live beyond the boundaries of pain and suffering and trauma. He will empower you to change.

You were meant to be morphed from natural into supernatural. You were meant to be changed from a low-crawling caterpillar into a high-flying butterfly. You were meant to transform from a weak man or woman with no ability to change the world into an incredibly strong Marvel-like superhero with the ability to help the hurting and change your environment for the better.

This is why this book is not only my story. It also is yours.

Call to Flight

At this time, I'd like to ask if you are a believer. Have you received Jesus Christ as your Lord and Savior? If so, I ask that you further implement change in the world around you by taking this story, this book, and putting it in the hands of someone around you who may be hurting.

Put it in the hands of someone whose life you believe God could change in this season. If you downloaded the book digitally, talk about it, share it verbally, explaining to someone else about the story of the convicted killer who was changed by the unconditional love of Christ. Then they too can pursue being morphed from the low place of a natural man or woman into the high place of a man or woman of God.

And if you have not yet received Jesus Christ as your Lord and Savior… Then I want to speak directly to you now.

Know that you are currently in an unnatural condition, locked in a state of pain, and paralysis by the lies you've been told and the trauma you've experienced.

But God said in 2 Corinthians 5:17 that if any man (or woman) be in Christ, they become a new creature.

I want to give you that opportunity right now. The opportunity to become a new creature by receiving Jesus Christ as your Lord and Savior.

If you'll speak these words out loud, I have prayed for you, and I trust God to not only make His change in you but to overpower those old lies and free you completely to fulfill His purpose. Can I have the great honor of leading you into the open arms of *The God* who *loves* you? You'll be free to embrace the high life He's called you to live the instant you say "Amen" at the end of this prayer…

Pray this out loud and say:

> *Father God, today in Jesus's name, I choose to receive Your forgiveness. I believe that Jesus paid the price for my sin, so I could be reconciled to You and be made brand new. I choose to give You my life wholeheartedly now, so You can do something with it. I recognize Jesus as my Savior, and as the Lord of my life. I repent of my sins, and I forgive those who've wronged me. Fill me now, Father God, with Your precious Holy Spirit.*
>
> *I thank You that Jesus died for my sins and rose from the dead, so I could die to sin and have everlasting life. I declare now that in Jesus's name I am born-again and made righteous in Him. From today on, I begin the process of permitting Your super inside of my natural to be revealed. I declare that those who saw me in the midst of my pain will later see me absolutely changed.*
>
> *In Jesus's mighty name. Amen.*

If you prayed that prayer, I congratulate you! Welcome to the family! You just made an eternal decision—a decision, which guarantees God's grace, mercy, and supernatural power will create change in your life, in the life of your family, and the lives of those around you.

Something has changed. Something is being morphed. That something is *you.*

Congratulations, the level change you have now experienced isn't temporary—it's eternal. Arise and shine! Answer

His call! I am praying for you and expecting God to release you from all that has kept you in bondage, to give you joy and peace on your journey, and for Him to gain great glory from your story.

As He will continue to gain from mine.

If you prayed this prayer aloud and meant it, I would love to add your name to my specific list of people to regularly pray for. Email me your name and born-again birth date (the day you prayed this) to 1morphedlife@gmail.com and let's agree for God's best in your life.

REFERENCES

"Behold." 2019. Oxford Online Dictionary. Lexico.Com. 2019. https://www.lexico.com/en/definition/behold.

"Morph." 2019a. Oxford Online Dictionary. Lexico. Com. 2019. https://www.lexico.com/en/definition/morph.

"Morph." 2019b. Merriam-Webster's Unabridged Dictionary. Merriam-Webster, Inc. 2019. https://www.merriam-webster.com/dictionary/morph.

The Holy Bible: King James Version [KJV]. 1999. New York: American Bible Society. Public Domain. https://www.biblegateway.com/versions/King-James-Version-KJV-Bible/#booklist

The Holy Bible: New Living Translation [NLT]. 1996, 2994, 2997, 2013. Tyndale House Foundation. Carol Stream, Illinois: Tyndale House Publishers, Inc.

The Holy Bible: The New King James Version [NKJV]. 1999, Nashville: Thomas Nelson. https://www.biblegateway.com/versions/New-King-James-Version-NKJV-Bible/#booklist

The Holy Bible: The World English Web [WEB]. 2000. Rainbow Missions. Public Domain. https://www.biblegateway.com/versions/World-English-Bible-WEB/#vinfo

Strong, James. 2010. *Jerusalem. Strong's Expanded Exhaustive Concordance of the Bible.* Expanded e. Thomas Nelson.

"Symptom." 2019. Oxford Online Dictionary. Lexico. Com. 2019. https://www.lexico.com/en/definition/symptom.

ABOUT THE AUTHOR

Artis (Free Man) Nelson has been a minister since 2006. He and his wife Tamichole are associate pastors at Life Change Church in Seattle, Washington. Artis is active in the present move of God and is the producer of the ministry television show. He also sits as pastor over the Recovery Meeting ministry team and is the director of Life Change House, a transitional housing ministry that oversees homeless individuals and those returning to society from prison. His profound revelation of the Word of God is taught with simplicity and clarity from a fresh and proven biblical perspective. Traveling both in America and internationally, Artis has been used by God to impact the lives of many. He and his wife live in Bellevue, Washington and are the loving parents of Artonique, Artis II, and Artiana Nelson.